Hawai'i in Love

by Toni Polancy

Photos by Matthew Thayer

Barefoot Publishing: *Practical Books About Paradise*
Kihei, Hawai'i

I

Parts of this book suggest ideas and resources for fun on the islands. They should be read as suggestions only. The author and Barefoot Publishing accept no responsibility for results, problems or accidents resulting from any of the suggestions in these book. Anyone venturing on a hike or a swim should use extreme caution, especially in Hawai'i's changeable weather, its dangerous cliffs and wild surf.

No money or gratuities of any kind were accepted from any of the resorts or restaurants mentioned in these pages. They represent the choices and preferences of the author and people she interviewed and should not be considered an endorsement. Also, prices, events, phone numbers or times quoted may have changed, and probably will have changed, during the life of this book.

Hawai'i In Love
True stories of island romance

This book is dedicated to all the lovers, alive and deceased, god and human, anonymous and otherwise, whose stories appear in its pages. Thank you for telling us, for teaching us, for helping us attempt to unravel the wonderful mystery of love.

INSIDE

Imagine...

Then came missionaries

And now us

And now us – continued

Resources for romance

Early Hawaiian lovers,
it is said,
"kissed"
without kissing.
A lover
showed affection
by drawing his beloved
to him and trading breaths,
gently laying
his face next to hers,
touching
cheeks,
inhaling
her very essence.

Imagine a land, sensuous and warm,

where desires dance untamed,

no strings — and no sins — attached.

A place where lovers rendezvous on rainbows;

where plants have passion,

rocks can copulate,

and gods occasionally mate with mortals.

Taro, a passionate plant

If plants are alive and grow, Hawaiian legend says, then surely they lead lives and have wills. And so it follows that trees and shrubs and even small plants can love each other.

Once, two beautifully formed taro plants fell in love. When a chief decided to serve them up at a feast, the frightened plants moved to another part of the garden. Later the chief again wanted to pick them and the pair again escaped. They continued moving about in the garden until there was no longer anywhere to hide and the chief nearly caught them. The leafy lovers then took wing and began moving from garden to garden to elude the chief's grasp. Finally a sympathetic farmer hid the trembling taros in his garden, where they lived happily ever after, spawning great watery patches of taro, a most important food in Hawai'i.

Want to increase your love's desire? Pick taro and pound its roots into poi, then feed it to your lover in the moonlight. ☂

MATTHEW THAYER PHOTO

2

Searching for true affection?
Like the god Oro, you too may find

Love at the end of a rainbow

One day, long long ago, the handsome Polynesian god Oro came to earth searching for true love. Accompanied by his two sisters, he arrived at the island of Bora Bora and began attending all the festivals where women gathered.

After several celebrations, he began to lament that true love did not exist for him. Finally, he spied a woman bathing in a tropical pool. She was so beautiful that Oro was overcome with longing for her and sent his sisters to ask if she would mate with him.

The young woman listened as the goddesses described Oro's desire for her. They explained that he was a young, handsome chieftain, but they did not tell the woman, whose name was Vairaumati, that Oro was a god.

Vairaumati agreed to make love with Oro, provided she was also attracted to him and her attraction grew to desire. The sisters arranged for Oro and Vairaumati to meet. Oro was all Vairaumati had been promised and more. They made love throughout that night and for many nights thereafter.

Each night, Oro descended to earth on a rainbow to visit his love.

To this day, the rainbow is a symbol of love in the Hawaiian islands. 🌴

3

Gods, goddesses and mortal matings

Hawaiians believed that *'aumakua*, friendly spirits of the dead, could fall in love and have intercourse with living persons. The *'aumakua* might choose a particularly comely mortal man or woman and come courting in a dream, making love with the sleeping mortal and sometimes even producing *keiki* or children.

Romantic? Yes.

Harmless? No.

Problems arose when either partner, corporeal or spirit, became too enthralled with the other. The human partner might become so lovelorn that he or she refused to eat, grew sick and died from love. Or, an over-emotional spirit-lover might actually coax the human to die and join the spirit world so they could be together.

It was safest to nip such nocturnal couplings in the bud ... or rather in the flower. The flower sheath of a banana plant, placed between the mortal's legs, became a kind of large, magical condom. Uncomfortable as this was, it stopped the dreamy trysts.

Still, some unearthly affairs had happy endings. One legend says a woman who had trouble conceiving a child dreamed of a man, resembling her husband, who came out of the sea and visited her at night. Each time she dreamed, she became pregnant.

Hawaiian folklore includes several stories of human-mortal love, some of which follow. 🌴

Few lovers would go to the depths
Hiku did to save his Kawelu

A tale of undying love

The young demigod Hiku lived with his mother on an isolated mountain summit on the island of Hawai'i. Hiku often heard music and alluring sounds from the villages below and he longed to follow the sounds.

His desire grew as he reached manhood and Hiku decided to descend to the enticing mortal world. His mother feared for him. Gods were powerful, but the mortal world was fraught with danger. What if Hiku were to fall in love with a mortal woman? Such matings rarely came to good for either party. His mother finally agreed to Hiku's journey, but made him promise not to stay away long.

At a village celebration, innocent Hiku laid eyes upon the lovely mortal princess Kawelu. She smiled upon Hiku and showed him pleasures he had never before known.

The happy couple spent several lustful days and nights together, but Hiku was bothered by the vow he had made to his mother. He told Kawelu he must return to his mother as he had promised. Unfortunately, what had begun as a simple flirtation for Kawelu had turned into a deep, abiding love. She missed Hiku so much that within a few days she died of a broken heart.

When Hiku returned to Kawelu's village, he was griefstricken. His first and only love was dead. Hiku mourned... but then he devised a plan. He would descend into the nether world, the world of the dead, to reclaim Kawelu's spirit.

Hiku convinced the young men of Kawelu's village to help him. Hoping to fool the deceased inhabitants of the netherworld into believing he also was dead, he anointed himself with a mixture of rancid coconut and *kukui* oil, which gave him a strong, corpse-like odor.

Hiku and his friends paddled their canoes to a point where the sky meets the water. There, they used a long vine to lower Hiku into the spirit world deep below the sea. The ruse worked; souls in the great cavern of death believed he was one of them.

Kawelu was pleased to see him, but she was sad that he, like she, had died. Hiku embraced Kawelu, but did not tell her of his plan. He had brought a large swing and he put her on it. Making it appear as a game, he swung Kawelu higher and higher until finally he lifted her spirit up into the world of the living. With his beloved's spirit captured in a coconut shell, he rushed to the house where her body lay and forced her reluctant spirit into a hole in the toe of her foot, massaging until her spirit had traveled throughout her body.

The loving massage worked. Kawelu revived and the couple lived happily ever after.

Ah! But departed spirits, once deceived, never forgive. Even today, Big Island residents report seeing the Night Marchers, ghosts in full Hawaiian dress that are messengers from the netherworld, mournfully trekking the swamps at night in search of the spirit of Kawelu. 🌴

'A 'ohe loa i ka hana a ke aloha.
Distance is ignored by love.

A warring god,

Kū makes a great sacrifice for his mortal wife

Gods were often warlike, demanding and capricious, but even the warring god Kū had a sensitive side. According to Polynesian legend Kū, who loved a mortal woman, performed an act of love that was truly selfless.

In Puna on the Big Island, Kū lived happily for several years with his human spouse, producing many half-mortal, half-god children. But then a devastating famine came. Food was scarce, his children grew thin and the family suffered greatly. Realizing that his children were starving, Kū made a great sacrifice. He said farewell to his mate and went into the garden. There, he stood on his head and as she watched, sobbing, he sank slowly into the ground until his entire body disappeared.

For days, the widow lingered in the garden mourning her beloved, crying so hard that her tears watered the place where he had disappeared.

One day, the sorrowing widow noticed that a plant sprouted where her tears had fallen. Rapidly the plant grew into a large tree that bore round green-gold globes of fruit. The strange fruit was thick-skinned with a soft, creamy center. Kū's sacrifice had spawned *ulu*, the prolific breadfruit tree. The woman shared the fruit with her neighbors, and they with their neighbors, and before long the abundant fruit had ended Hawai'i's famine.

Today, breadfruit still grows profusely, providing an inexpensive, potato like staple for Hawaiian tables. It is said that a breadfruit tree in your yard ensures your family will never starve or suffer as Kū's family did. 🌴

He punawai kahe wale ke aloha
Love is a spring that flows freely

Care to conceive?
Come spend a night at

The mating rock of Moloka'i

Polynesians believed stones and rocks contained mystical powers, as well as genders. Appropriately, smooth, upright rocks were male. Flatter, more porous rocks were female.

Stones could also give birth. Placing a male stone with a female stone under the right conditions resulted in the birth of pebbles, which could grow up to be boulders.

Some rocks contained powerful fertility *mana*, or spirit. Male rocks, remarkably phallic, could also be fertility shrines. Hawai'i's most famous example, Kauleonānāhoa (literally "the penis of Nānāhoa") is a massive clump of lava at Pālā'au State Park on the island of Moloka'i. Legend says the six-foot shaft which never loses its rigidity was once a man named Nānāhoa. He had angered the gods by abusing his wife, so they turned him to stone.

Infertile women wishing to conceive brought offerings and spent prayerful nights at the base of "Phallic Rock." They were pregnant the next morning.

And even to this day, it is whispered, the sensuous stone welcomes desperate midnight visitors. 🌴

Flower of love

The resilient *naupaka* flower, with its pretty half-flower blossom, symbolizes lovers tragically separated. According to Hawaiian lore, a young couple was forbidden by their parents to wed. Broken-hearted, the girl plucked a *naupaka* blossom from its bush, tore the flower in half and, giving one half to her lover, fled to the mountains.

So one lover was banished into the mountains and the other to the ocean's sandy shore and each was forever thinking of the other, striving to be reunited. Like the separated lovers, the *naupaka* flower thrives both in dry sand and hard earth, producing strong, beautiful flowers. But it is forever creeping closer to shore, striving to be united with its heart's desire.

If you should find a whole *naupaka* flower, be thankful. It means the lovers are finally together. You and your lover will also be reunited. 🌴

A goddess scorned

G. BRAD LEWIS PHOTO

One night Pele, Hawai'i's most revered goddess, mistress of the Big Island's volcanoes, fell into a deep sleep and her spirit left her body.

Following the music of a whistle and a flute, her spirit arrived at the far-off island of Kaua'i, where Pele saw for the first time Lohi'au, the handsome young chief of Kaua'i. Pele immediately fell in love and, taking the form of a beautiful hula dancer, she seduced Lohi'au.

The couple enjoyed just three glorious nights together before Pele had to return to the Big Island. Since she was a spirit, it was as easy for her to travel as it is for the evening breezes to blow. But it would be dangerous for Lohi'au to traverse the treacherous ocean and islands, inhabited by gods who would be angry that Pele had mated with a mortal. She asked him to wait for her, vowing to send someone to help him make the journey.

Her trusted sister, Hi'iaka, who had been watching over Pele's inert body as the goddess visited the human world, was relieved to see Pele return to spirit consciousness. Pele told Hi'iaka of her adventure and sent her to get Lohi'au, warning her not to fall in love with the handsome mortal. Pele gave her sister just 40 days to return with Lohi'au. Meanwhile, she readied a home for him on the Big Island.

Faithful to her sister's wishes, Hi'iaka used wit and power to overcome many dangers and her journey to Kaua'i is one of Hawai'i's great legends. But the journey took so long that Lohi'au died of longing for his beautiful Pele. Hi'iaka was awestruck when she first beheld the body of the handsome Lohi'au. How could a mere mortal be so comely? She restored his life and soon, as her sister Pele had feared, Hi'iaka fell in love with the young chief.

> *I manai kau,*
> *i pua hoʻi*
> *kaʻu,*
> *kuiʻia ka*
> *makemake a*
> *lawa pono.*

Yours the lei-making needle, mine the flowers; so let us do as we wish (make a complete lei).

You, the man, and I, the woman; let us satisfy the demands of love. (Said by Hiʻaka in a chant as she embraced Lohiʻau at the rim of Kilauea to rouse the jealous wrath of Pele.)

From *Olelo Noʻeau: Hawaiian proverbs & poetical sayings* by Mary Kawena Pukui © 1983 Bishop Museum Press.

However, faithful to her sister, Hiʻiaka resisted temptation.

As Pele had foreseen, her god-relatives were angry that she had mated with a mortal, and they made Hiʻiaka and Lohiʻau's return journey long and perilous. Pele's 40-day limit passed, and then more days went by, and still her beloved husband and sister did not return. At first concerned, Pele grew more and more angry, sure Hiʻiaka and Lohiʻau had made love. In a fit of fury, Pele sent thick black lava oozing over Hiʻiaka's favorite forest. One of Hiʻiaka's dearest friends lived in the forest and the flaming lava killed her.

Meanwhile, the pair had indeed fallen in love, but they remained faithful to Pele. Long past the 40-day deadline, tired and exhausted from the perilous trip, the couple finally arrived on the Big Island. Fearing Pele's temper, Hiʻiaka sent two friends to explain to Pele why the journey had taken so long. Furious, Pele refused to listen. In her anger, she overwhelmed the friends with fire, killing them. Only then did Hiʻiaka, for the first time and on the edge of a volcanic crater in full view of her sister, accept Lohiʻau's embraces. Enraged, Pele called upon members of her family to consume Lohiʻau in fire but, struck by the young man's beauty, they pitied him. Finally, Pele herself encircled the lovers with fire. Hiʻiaka had a divine body and could not be hurt, but Lohiʻau was consumed by flames. Grieving, Hiʻiaka, through more brave deeds, was finally able to restore his life. The couple lived happily ever after, even until today, even as Pele continues to exhibit her wrath in a continual outpouring of jealous fire such as that of the volcano Kīlauea on the Big Island. 🌴

*Tattoos like these are
popular today. But
they were once
worn for protection.*

Tattoo:
The mark
of safety

*Wedding rings: a modern twist
on finger tattoos.*

Among the many immigrants who came to work on Hawai'i's plantations
were the Okinawans. For many generations Okinawan women tattooed the
tops of their fingers and hands to indicate they were married. Legend says this
is how the custom began:

A beautiful Okinawan princess was kidnapped and held captive by a
powerful Japanese lord. Knowing that Japanese looked down on body
markings, the princess tattooed the tops of her hands and fingers.

Appalled by the dark markings, the lord released her.

Later, young Okinawan girls, fearing they would be captured by
Japanese pirates and sold as prostitutes, tattooed their hands so they would
be less desirable. 🌴

A mother's tears; a father's sobs

Mānoa Valley on the island of O'ahu is misty and mysterious, rimmed with rainbows and blessed with dewy rain. Legend says Mānoa's rains are the tears of a mourning mother and its soft winds the moans of a bereaved father.

Their beautiful daughter Kahala-o-puna was betrothed to Kauhi, a young chief. Although Kahala gave Kauhi no reason to be mistrustful, her beauty caused him to be jealous and suspicious. He accused Kahala of being unfaithful and, in fits of fury, killed her—not once, but five times. Each time her 'aumakua, guardian spirit, resurrected her. But the sixth time, the 'aumakua was unable to help Kahala and she lay dead.

Soon a young prince found her and, enchanted by her fairness, fell in love with her. He convinced his own 'aumakua to return her to life one last time. To protect Kahala, the spirits turned Kauhi into a shark, cursed to forever roam the ocean.

Kahala returned the young prince's affection and lived happily with him and her parents, who warned her never to go near the ocean where the shark Kauhi dwelled. For a time she heeded those warnings. But the cool ocean waves called to Kahala and one morning she waded at the water's edge. Then, unable to resist the ocean's lure, Kahala dove gracefully into the sea. The sea is huge, after all, and a shark small in comparison. Surely, Kauhi would not find her.

Delicate as a flower lei floating on a sleepy sea, lulled by gentle waves, she drifted farther and farther.

Ah, but watching from under the water was the shark Kauhi, who had long been swimming near the shore, waiting for such on opportunity. With his mighty jaws he seized Kahala and tore her to death—a seventh and final time.

So it is that to this day her parents, the misty rain and the gentle wind of Mānoa, mourn for the tragic Kahala-o-puna. And each morning for just a few hours, in the form of the sun's gentle rays, she visits the valley to console her loving parents. 🌴

Her father's anger imprisoned

The maiden
of the cave

The great warrior king Kamehameha came for fun and sport to the little island of Lāna'i. His favorite warriors accompanied him and the most fierce and handsome was the young chief Ka'aiali'i.

Adorned only in flowers, all the beautiful young maidens of Lāna'i greeted the king's party. Among them was Kaala, the fairest maiden of all, just 15 years old. Where the flowers and leis of leaves did not cover her, Kaala's glistening brown skin showed enticingly. Her innocent eyes were large and soft. Both Kamehameha and Ka'aiali'i were smitten by her beauty, but Kamehameha could see that Kaala returned Ka'aiali'i's affection and he gave their love his blessing.

However, a few years before, the king's warriors had fought a fierce battle on Lāna'i and in that battle Ka'aiali'i had killed the best friend of Kaala's father, Opuniu. Now, Opuniu was determined that Ka'aiali'i should not have his beautiful daughter.

"I have promised her to Mailou," he told Kamehameha. Called the bone-breaker, Mailou was a strong and violent man, known for his fighting skill. Mailou was also notorious for devouring the gentle spirit of young maidens, then casting them aside.

Kamehameha decided that Ka'aiali'i and Mailou would battle to see who should have Kaala. Kaala sobbed, sure that Mailou would kill Ka'aiali'i. But the young warrior was fast and strong. He broke first one, then the other of Mailou's arms, disabling him.

15

Now Kaala belonged to Ka'aiali'i and would return with him to the island of Hawai'i. The maiden joyfully became a woman in his arms that night. But Opuniu was furious that Ka'aiali'i had won the right to have his daughter.

The next day, Opuniu found the young lovers and asked Kaala to come with him to visit her mother, whom he claimed was dying. A kind young woman, Kaala said she would travel with Opuniu to see her mother if Ka'aiali'i agreed she should go.

"For no other reason would I be separated from you," Ka'aiali'i said. "But I love my mother and know you must love yours. So go, but return quickly to me that we may start our new life together."

Kaala twined her arms around Ka'aiali'i's neck and touched her cheek to his in the Hawaiian way of kissing. As Ka'aiali'i watched from high on a cliff, Kaala followed her father away, waving to Ka'aiali'i until she could see him no more.

Father and daughter travelled into the forest, into the interior of the island, then back toward the sea.

"You are not taking me to my mother," Kaala said. "Where are you taking me?"

Opuniu did not answer, but led his daughter to the very rocky edge of a cliff. Below, the angry sea boiled and leaped.

"I will not let Ka'aiali'i, the man who killed my friend, now take my daughter away from me, off the island of Lāna'i," Opuniu growled.

Clutching Kaala's wrist, Opuniu leaped from the cliff into the churning sea. He was strong and able to fight his way through the waves to a ledge just below the water. Dragging his terrified daughter along, he climbed through the rocks into a dark cave filled with blackened water. At the back of the dark cave was a narrow beach. Salt crystals hung from the cave's ceiling and large black crabs skittered across the rocks, stopping to stare boldly at the human pair.

"Until Kamehameha and his men have left Lāna'i and gone back to their own island, you will stay here," Opuniu told the shivering Kaala.

"Father! No! Please. I will die here. Please do not leave me here. The eels will sting me and the crabs will eat out my eyes. Please!"

Opuniu decided to give his daughter one more chance. "I will take you back up with me to the sunshine," said Opuniu, "if you will go to Olowalu to be with Mailou. If you will embrace him in front of your lover Ka'aiali'i, for him to see."

16

"Never," sobbed Kaala. "Never."

So cruel Opuniu left his daughter in that cursed place.

Ka'aiali'i waited for Kaala, watching the paths, listening for her footsteps, and he became more and more distraught when she did not return. One day, Ua, Kaala's dearest friend, came to Ka'aiali'i with the news that Opuniu had hidden Kaala away somewhere. Ua believed Opuniu had taken Kaala inland, which indeed he had, at first. So Kaalilii began to search the forest and the interior of Lāna'i, calling for his love.

Kamehameha, sad for his favorite warrior, urged Ka'aiali'i to forget Kaala. "Take her friend Ua instead," he said. "She is also beautiful and she loves you. I will make you chief of all Lāna'i and you will be happy here."

But Ka'aiali'i was sure he could love no one but Kaala and told the king so.

He continued searching and calling for Kaala. Eventually, he came to the ocean's edge and some mysterious force, perhaps the gods, led him to the same rocky cliff from which Opuniu had jumped with his daughter.

Ka'aiali'i stood on the cliff, staring down into the leaping water. In its forms and froth, he saw the shape of Kaala. In the mesmerizing sound of the tide he heard her voice, calling back to him.

Suddenly, he threw himself into the foaming ocean, between the rocks and near the ledge of a cave. He crawled inside and there he found his Kaala. She was thin and torn, hardly breathing, her skin beaten by waves and eaten by crabs.

"My Kaala," Ka'aiali'i exclaimed, clutching her soft, listless body to him. "I have found you. I will take you from here. I will save you."

But Kaala could barely speak.

"Oh my Ka'aiali'i, you have come. But it is too late. I am dying." Kaala used her last bit of strength to reach her little arms around his neck for a last, gentle embrace.

When he saw that his Kaala was dead, Ka'aiali'i sobbed aloud, calling out in sadness and frustration. Then, with all the mighty strength in his body, Ka'aiali'i dashed his own head against the rocks, killing himself.

So to this day the two lovers lie side by side in that sad, dark place, the Spouting Cave of Lāna'i. 🌴

Quite a crater . . .

Hawaiians had descriptive names for items and locations, and often those names were erotic. Perhaps the most fanciful is Kohelepelepe or "fringed vagina," an ancient name for Koko Crater on the island of Oʻahu. Legend says Kamapuaʻa, the pig god, attempted to ravish the goddess Pele. Pele's sister Kapo had a flying vagina that she could send where she willed. She sent it to tempt Kamapuaʻa. Fickle Kamapuaʻa saw the soaring sex object and, immediately releasing Pele, he followed the vagina to Koko Crater, where it landed, left an imprint, and flew on to Kalihi. Legend does not say what happened to it there.

A *kapu*, happily broken

In ancient Polynesia, menstruating women were considered unclean and were thus forbidden, *kapu*. They could not attend religious services, handle certain foods or perform many of their usual duties. And they might be secluded from their families, going to special village houses to wait out their ordeal in the company of other women. At this time of month, women did not indulge in sex with husbands or lovers.

After her menses had ceased, a woman would go to the sea and indulge in *kapu kai*, a ritual bath designed to cleanse the body and soul of any defilement. It was performed in private and the woman prayed as she bathed. Such ablutions, it was believed, were most effective if repeated for five consecutive days.

Between menstruation and cleansing baths, the taboo meant couples might abstain from sex for as long as ten or eleven days each month. While surely that might seem extensive to new lovers, the ritual, some women say, has benefits.

A woman married to a man from an island where such baths are still practiced highly defends the practice.

"Being away from each other for a time each month, being by yourself, replenishes the spirit," she states. "And the ritual bath becomes very sensual. A time to concentrate on your body and soul and prepare yourself for your mate. You perform the final bath, perhaps by moonlight, knowing he is waiting anxiously.

"And each month, your love is new and exciting." 🌴

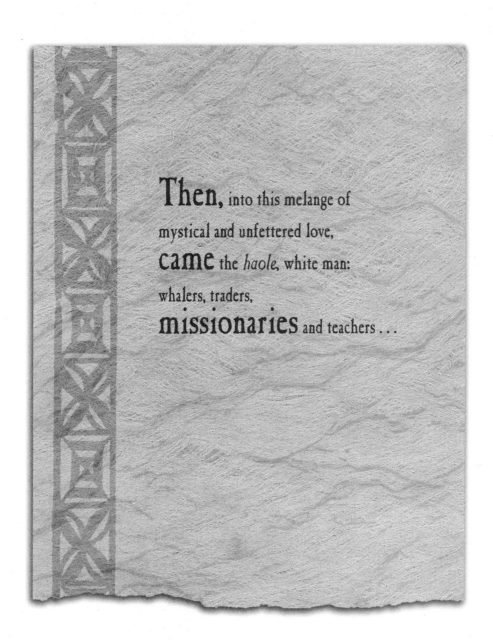

Then, into this melange of mystical and unfettered love, **came** the *haole*, white man: whalers, traders, **missionaries** and teachers . . .

Elizabeth Cook spent just four years with her

Wandering husband

Imagine being married to a man you love and sometimes not hearing from him for months or years at a time, being unsure he is even alive.

That was the fate of Elizabeth Batts of Essex County, England, who in 1762 married the famous explorer Captain James Cook. Much has been written about Captain Cook's explorations; but almost nothing is recorded about his marriage to Elizabeth, who may have been the perfect wife for such a wandering man. She knew what she was getting into when she married James, the poorly educated son of a farmer. He had shown himself to be a brilliant navigator and had already conducted successful explorations for the British admiralty.

Legend says James was godfather to Elizabeth, and at her baptism vowed that he would one day marry her. That story seems unlikely – he would have been only about 13 when she was born and they came from different backgrounds. However, since the Cooks' courtship was so short – hardly more than a few days – they may have had a previous relationship, unrecorded by history. James, it is said, was a patient, persevering man, and waiting for Elizabeth to grow to marriageable age would have been characteristic of him.

Elizabeth and James met (or remet) at Shadwell, England. He was 34, had just returned from successful expeditions to Nova Scotia and Newfoundland, and was already commissioned for other

journeys. Elizabeth, 21, was
visiting her mother and
stepfather.

After their wedding, the
couple bought a home at 88 Mile
End, Old Towne, London, and
Elizabeth settled in, seemingly
content with her wandering
husband. For much of the next
16 years, she lived quietly and
waited for his sporadic returns, as
James established himself as one
of history's greatest explorers.
Communication was poor in the
1700s and so she might not hear
of her husband for months or
years at a time. He was exploring
unknown parts of the world and
could easily be dead without her knowing.

Still, by all accounts, the Cooks' marriage was happy. Nearly every time
James came home, Elizabeth became pregnant, eventually giving birth to
three sons.

He was seeking a northern route to the Pacific Ocean in January 1779,
when his two ships, the *Resolution* and the *Discovery*, came upon the island of
Kaua'i. Friendly, though wary, natives paddled out in canoes to greet the
voyagers. They eagerly traded fish, pigs and sweet potatoes for brass and small
pieces of iron. Islanders, according to Cook's accounts, were tall, strong,
beautiful, warm, hospitable and frank, but given to stealing. In fact, they so
valued nails that they would swim under the ships to pluck nails from the ships'
hulls.

Cook's exploration of Kaua'i, Maui and the Big Island marked the beginning
of the outside world's influence in the islands. Within the next 70 years Hawai'i
would play host – and prey – to whalers and traders, pirates and priests.

Eventually foreigners became known in the islands as *haole*, and legend says the name took hold during Cook's visits. Polynesians greeted each other by trading breaths, exhaling into one another's faces. Cook's men were understandably reluctant to trade breath with the natives and so they were called *haole*, which can be translated as "without breath."

The crew may have been reluctant to trade breaths, but they were more than willing to trade another commodity: sex. Island culture had few sexual boundaries. Lovemaking came as easily and naturally to the natives as, well, breathing. Mating was open and casual and the resulting children belonged to, and were raised by the village or community.

Native women were eager to share their affections. They swam out to the ships full of men who had long been away from the comforts of home. Cook, aware that some of his men carried venereal disease, at first tried to limit contact, but soon the women were spending days and nights on board. History pays little attention to whether or not Cook himself participated in the love fests. At one point after his death, island storytellers had him mating with a Hawaiian princess, but historical documents show no such record.

The Hawaiian voyage eventually brought James to his death. His ships had arrived on the Big Island during the winter celebration of *Makahiki*, a tribute to the god Lono. Unknown to Cook, the natives thought he was Lono. When he returned to that island a few weeks later, *Makahiki* had ended and they realized he was a mortal man. For reasons still unclear, the Hawaiians turned on him and his crew retaliated with gunfire. Cook was stabbed and killed in a skirmish at Kealakekua Bay on the island of Hawai'i on February 14, 1779. He was 51.

Elizabeth would not learn of her husband's death for many months, until ships brought the story back to England. In recognition of James' contributions in both exploration and astronomy, the king granted her a pension and she lived on for many years. She never remarried. Subtracting the time James Cook was away, Elizabeth had spent little more than four years with her beloved husband. 🌴

The marriages of Hawai'i's first missionaries were matters of necessity.

God plays matchmaker

The year was 1819. Hiram Bingham, tall and strong, paced his small room, hands behind his back, a frown on his sensitive face. At the age of 29, he had a serious problem. Sarah, the fiancé he had courted for three months, changed her mind and would not marry him.

It is bad enough for any fiancé to be rejected, but Hiram had special reasons to be upset. He was the leader of a group of young missionaries scheduled to embark on a long journey to Owhyhee, today's Hawai'i. The men had heard stories of naked natives worshipping pagan gods, frolicking in the sea and sharing sexual favors with whalers and traders in those far-off islands. They had all volunteered to teach the word and ways of the Christian God to the shameless heathens.

Great temptation awaited the young men. The American Board of Commissioners for Foreign Missions, who recruited them, stipulated that before setting out on their journey, the missionaries must marry "girls of known piety."

Now, here I am, Hiram thought, *due to sail in less than a month, with no wife and no prospects of one.*

His fellow missionaries were more fortunate. One was already married and, through the grace of God and the help of friends, five other bachelors soon found women willing to leave family and friends behind and embark on a five-month-long voyage to start a new life in a far-off godless land. It was a bit embarrassing for Hiram, their leader, to be the only minister still wife-less.

There was one thing he could do – bring the problem to Him who solves all problems. Hiram would leave it up to God to supply a wife.

The weeks sped by. Soon it was the day of the young men's ordination. And still Hiram had no bride. Would God let him down? Must he withdraw from the mission?

Among those planning to attend the ordination was a young woman named Sybil Mosely. She had been so inspired by tales of the missionaries' forthcoming journey that she traveled several hundred miles—a long and tiresome trip in those days —to wish them well.

Most likely, Sybil secretly hoped to marry one of the men. For several years, she had been teaching school, one of the few professions open to women in 1819, and her diary says she had been searching and praying for more stimulating endeavors. In fact, Sybil had been courted by at least two missionaries before meeting Hiram. She had rejected the first young man, and the second, whom she had nearly wed, was sent to a part of the world where the Board allowed only bachelors.

Introduced by friends, Sybil asked Hiram for directions to the ceremony and he offered to drive her there in a buggy. As they rode along, they began to talk. Sybil knew what lay ahead for Hiram, but he must have been surprised to find that this delicate-looking woman would gladly consider joining him on his journey – both to Hawai'i and through life.

At the last moment, God had answered both their prayers. Here, surely, was a match made in heaven.

Hiram and Sybil wed on October 11, three weeks after they met, and just in time to board the brig *Thaddeous*. The *Thaddeous* would cross two oceans with its 23 passengers and 20 crew members, and travel for 164 days. Small and cramped, the ship offered little privacy and few opportunities for the couples to become better acquainted. Worse, they traversed the Pacific Ocean at the stormiest time of the year; seasickness compounded their miseries. Still, no matter how rough the seas or how dangerous the journey, it was a honeymoon of sorts. Among the seven couples, four wives delivered children within nine months of their landing. 🌴

From the time they were born,
this prince and princess believed
they were destined to wed.

A brother and sister in love

A young man and woman walk in the shadows at the Honolulu wharf, holding hands, gazing out at the moon's reflection on the water and murmuring intensely. Suddenly the young man kisses the young woman, deeply and ardently.

"Wait here!" he whispers. "I will return."

He quickly disappears, lost in the shadows.

She waits. And waits. But he does not come back.

The young woman is Princess Nāhi'ena'ena. The young man is her brother, Prince Kauikeaouli, and they are tragically caught in a war between conflicting religions and cultures.

Princess Nāhi'ena'ena and Prince Kauikeaouli, just two years apart in age, were the youngest children of Hawai'i's greatest warrior/king Kamehameha the Great and his wife Keōpūolani. Pampered and catered to by bevies of servants from the time they were born, the children believed they were specially endowed by the gods and that they were destined to marry each other.

It is hard to imagine how very royally the little prince and princess were treated. Nāhi'ena'ena was only eight years old when her eldest brother Liholiho ascended to the throne in 1823. She arrived at his inaugural celebration in a decorated carriage, drawn not by horses, but by her servants and friends. A few days later, she came to another function on a servant's shoulders, followed by a train of thirty boys and girls, and she was dressed as a European child, in satins and laces, wearing a hat with feathers.

Each royal child had his own house and servants, so Nāhiʻenaʻena and Kauikeaouli lived apart, yet they played together often and were fond of each other, believing they would spend their lives together. But soon Nāhiʻenaʻena's life changed dramatically. Her mother became very ill and moved from the busy Honolulu court to quieter Lahaina, Maui, where Nāhiʻenaʻena was placed under the tutelage of strict missionaries. As her health worsened, Keōpūolani decided to be the first person of royal blood to be baptized in the new faith. Before she died, she asked the missionaries to make sure her children were educated as Christians.

Suddenly the spoiled princess was forced to learn the precepts of a new religion, one that sanctioned piety and purity over pomp and pageantry.

For the next few years, as she grew into a very pretty young woman, Nāhiʻenaʻena led a dual life. She was a student, treated much as a commoner, told when to rise and when to sleep, when to study and when and what to eat, bowing to the wishes of teachers and her new God. She was also a princess, still attending royal functions and appearing in church in fancy European satins, attended by a retinue of servants and friends.

The royal children commemorated the death of their mother by staging a grand pageant in which Nāhiʻenaʻena dazzled the

28

admiring multitudes by appearing in a succession of splendid robes. The ensuing banquet ended in wild drunkenness. Then, Nāhiʻenaʻena went off with a native priest to sacrifice to the old gods. Next, she became again a devout Christian. At a women's church meeting, she led the congregation in prayers.

At one point, Nāhiʻenaʻena's followers fashioned for her a magnificent skirt from rare yellow bird feathers. Tradition called for her to be bare to her waist as she wore the opulent skirt. Missionaries urged modesty and so to satisfy both the old world and the new, Nāhiʻenaʻena wore a European dress under the skirt. The battle for Nāhiʻenaʻena's soul and spirit would haunt her life.

Hawaiian chiefs (*aliʻi*), concerned about preserving royal blood lines in rapidly changing Hawaiʻi, wanted Nāhiʻenaʻena and Kauikeaouli to wed, as it had long been assumed they would. In fact, it was rumored that the prince and princess already slept together. But missionaries refused to allow what they considered an incestuous marriage.

In 1827, Nāhiʻenaʻena, 12, was accepted as a full-fledged member of the Christian church, and for a time she was devoted to her new faith. But then Kauikeaouli became king and before long rumors abounded that he led a life of drunken debauchery. Nāhiʻenaʻena was said to be living in sin with her brother. She denied this to the missionaries and, over the next few years, she alternated bouts of drinking, card playing and pursuing pleasures

with her brother with periods of resolute remorse and a return to missionary tenets.

Meanwhile, the young king sank further into sin with his gang of followers. Was this because the natural course of his life, marriage to his sister Nāhiʻenaʻena, was denied him? History can only guess.

The *aliʻi*, concerned about their king, sent for Nāhiʻenaʻena. She tried to persuade her brother to come to Lahaina with her.

That is how the couple came to be strolling, hand-in-hand, to the Honolulu wharf, where they were to board a ship to Lahaina. She waited and waited, but Kauikeaouli did not come back. Instead, he left the weeping Nāhiʻenaʻena at the wharf.

Later, remorseful, he sent a ship to bring her to him at his country retreat in Oʻahu. When she refused to go, Kauikeaouli attempted suicide, but his life was saved.

Finally, Nāhiʻenaʻena agreed to marry her brother according to Hawaiian custom, by sleeping together in the presence of their chiefs. When a crier spread the word through town, the missionaries were horrified. This time, Nāhiʻenaʻena was excommunicated from the church.

Again, she grew contrite and the missionaries decided to find her a mate. They arranged for her to marry Leleiōhuku, a ward of the governor of Hawaiʻi. Nāhiʻenaʻena sailed for Kona where she was wed in a grand celebration, but the marriage did not accomplish what the missionaries had hoped. Nāhiʻenaʻena never returned to the church.

In 1836, when he learned that she was pregnant, her brother came to take Nāhiʻenaʻena to Honolulu for the royal birth. On September 17 a son was born, but he died within hours.

Just a few months later, on December 30, Nāhiʻenaʻena died. She was just 21 years old. Her beloved brother was at her bedside. 🌴

Awaiaulu ke aloha
Love made fast by tying together: marriage

Who exhibits the greater love? The foreigner who pursues
a princess despite the objections of her royal family?
Or the young prince who releases her from marital promises?

One princess, two fiancés

It was the custom among Hawaiians, not so long ago, to give young children to revered relatives to raise as *hānai* or adopted children. This special act of obedience and love took much sacrifice on the part of the new parents.

Bernice Pauahi, dainty and fair-skinned, was born in 1831 of noble lineage, and was immediately given as *hānai* daughter to her aunt Kinaʻu, oldest daughter of Kamehameha the Great, Hawaiʻi's most renowned king.

Kinaʻu decided that when she was old enough Pauahi would marry one of Kinaʻu's own three sons. She chose Lot, the middle son. And if Lot were to die, Pauahi was to marry his younger brother, Alexander.

Pauahi was raised as a princess, lovingly cared for by a retinue of *kahu*, or attendants. But Kinaʻu was wise and kind, and Pauahi grew up in this royal household learning that privilege included responsibility. She must love her subjects and make careful decisions on their behalf.

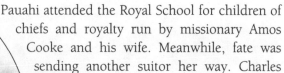

Pauahi attended the Royal School for children of chiefs and royalty run by missionary Amos Cooke and his wife. Meanwhile, fate was sending another suitor her way. Charles Reed Bishop arrived in Honolulu in 1846. A store clerk, he had left New York to find his fortune in Oregon or California. He and a friend visited Hawai'i, where they were welcomed by other *haoles* (foreigners) and learned that their mainland savvy would take them far in the islands. Charles' friend was made a judge and Charles obtained a job with the government, overseeing the foreclosure of Hawai'i's first sugar company. Next, he was given a position as U.S. Consulate. Pauahi was about 16 and Charles 24 when they met at

Charles Reed Bishop

an evening get-together at the school. Charles, handsome and daring, had an outgoing personality. Pauahi, an intelligent and accomplished musician, was the most beautiful of the royal children. Soon he began to visit regularly to catch another glimpse of Pauahi.

Charles continued to call at the school for two years, and the journal of schoolmaster Amos Cooke indicates he eventually asked to be allowed to court (or wed) Pauahi. His suit was discouraged. Perhaps overcome with anger or grief, he considered leaving Hawai'i, where he had begun to make wise and successful business investments. But then he was offered a position as Collector of Customs and so he became a citizen, swearing allegiance to the King. Hawai'i would become his permanent home.

Now Charles was able to convince the Cookes that his affection for Pauahi was genuine. They questioned Pauahi and, assured that she returned Charles' love, they decided to take the young couple's side in what would be a long ordeal: persuading her parents, royal relatives, kingly advisers and thousands of subjects that Pauahi should break with tradition and wed a man who was a foreigner, a newcomer and a commoner with little money or background.

Pauahi may have been shy with strangers, but she could also be bold and determined. Once she decided to marry Charles, she let nothing stand in her way. First, she went to her *hānai* father, the governor, and told him politely but firmly that she did not want to marry his son Lot.

Angered, her relatives pressured Pauahi to announce her engagement to Lot immediately. The fact that she loved someone else meant little to the family. Marriage was a matter of politics and honor, of strengthening blood ties. It was not to be wasted in love.

Distressed almost to the point of illness, Pauahi went to Prince Lot and said she did not love him. Nor, she declared, did he

Prince Lot (Kamehameha V)

love her. Throughout his childhood Lot had assumed that he and Pauahi would wed and he greatly admired her, so it was not completely true that he did not love her, at least as a brother loves a sister. Her words may have hurt him, but he did not say so.

Next Pauahi wrote a letter to her *hānai* father saying she would abide by her family's wishes, but it would mean her death. She was not threatening suicide; she meant as Lot's wife she would slowly die from sorrow, a condition recognized in Hawaiian tradition.

It was Lot who, in a gesture of selfless love, saved Pauahi from such a living death. As soon as he saw the letter to his father, he officially and firmly, in writing, released Pauahi from all marital promises made for her during her youth. He wrote that he knew he was unworthy of Pauahi and referred to "one who was worthy" and said he hoped she would be happy.

The way was opened for Charles and Pauahi to wed, but their problems were far from over. Opposition to the marriage from family, *ali'i*, and Pauahi's subjects was intense. When Charles tried to get a marriage license he was told he could not do so without the approval of Pauahi's father, and for a time Pauahi's birth parents disowned her.

Despite the opposition, Charles Reed Bishop and Bernice Pauahi were finally wed in a quiet ceremony in the parlor of the royal school on the evening of Tuesday, June 4, 1850. Her family did not attend. After a simple supper, they went by carriage to a boarding house where they would live.

Despite the inauspicious start, fortune smiled – indeed, fortune beamed – on the couple. Pauahi's birth parents eventually forgave her and welcomed Charles into the family. The couple enjoyed more than 30 years of ideal marital happiness.

Charles took a leading role in the development of Hawai'i. He started the first successful bank in 1858, a forbearer of today's First Hawaiian Bank. Pauahi was the final heir to the royal lands of O'ahu. When she died, the lands she owned and some of Charles' own land was put into the Bishop Trust, created by her husband in her memory.

Today, the Bishop Estate, which at one time totalled 431,000 acres or one-ninth of Hawai'i, still controls much O'ahu land. The Bishop Museum, created by Charles to honor his wife and her Hawaiian culture, still welcomes hundreds of visitors daily. And the Kamehameha Schools, funded by the Bishop Estate, provide education to children of Hawaiian lineage.

These are enduring memorials to a couple who deeply loved each other. And, in a way, they also honor Prince Lot, who so unselfishly released his betrothed from her commitment.

Prince Lot, as the visionary King Kamehameha V, would rule the islands for nine years, launching the tourist industry by building Hawai'i's first large hotel, the Royal Hawaiian. He also started the Royal Hawaiian Band, which still serenades Honolulu visitors and residents.

Hawaiians, isolated by an ocean, had little resistance to the illnesses the world brought. Diseases and infections claimed thousands, among them much of the Kamehameha royal line—and finally Prince Lot, who suffered a fatal chest infection.

On his death bed, Lot asked Bernice Pauahi Bishop to assume a role she might have had as his queen, to be his successor. She gently declined. Prince Lot died a few minutes later, leaving Hawai'i temporarily without a monarch. He was 42 years old and had never wed. 🌴

Love was sometimes consummated in tears at

Honolulu's Hotel of Sorrows

In the early 1900s, there was a hotel near the wharf in Honolulu that some called the Hotel of Sorrows. It was said that if you walked by this particular hotel on certain evenings, you could hear sobs emanating from the rooms.

The lamentations occurred only on nights after a ship had arrived bringing "picture brides" to Hawai'i from Asia.

By the 1880s, Hawai'i's large sugar and pineapple plantations needed workers. Lured by hopes of a better life and decent wages, men were recruited from around the world – Portugal, Japan, Korea, China and other countries.

Many of the plantation workers were unwed Asian men who came hoping to earn money and eventually return to their own countries. But after years on the plantation and realizing they might never go home, some asked families and friends to send them wives. Prospective brides and grooms exchanged photos – the blurry sepia images of early cameras – and chose mates without ever actually meeting.

Arranging "picture bride" marriages became an avocation for match-makers in Asia and a business for entrepreneurs in Hawai'i. Matchmakers received a handsome fee for their services. And the photographer who snapped photos of plantation workers might even rent them suits so that they could appear more prosperous. Occasionally, a middle-aged or homely man might be concerned that no woman would choose him. Rather than take a chance on finding a match, he might ask a younger or better-looking man to stand in for him in the photograph. The photos were sent off to relatives and matchmakers in the homeland.

In many parts of Asia, women were an expendable commodity and had no choice in the matter. Families would arrange the marriages for a variety of reasons. Some simply hoped for better lives for their daughters. They had been led to believe that anyone who lived in Hawai'i was prosperous.

In truth, most plantation workers endured long, sweltering hours in Hawai'i's pineapple and sugar fields for low wages – and they expected their new wives to also work in the fields while still caring for a house and family.

The grooms, and sometimes the matchmakers, stood on the O'ahu docks, awaiting the ships. Each man, holding his bride's picture, peered into the faces of the women demurely leaving the ship. Sometimes the couples recognized each other and smiled shyly. Sometimes they were so unlike their pictures that the matchmaker had to introduce them.

Mass marriages often took place right at the dock. Some couples went immediately to their new homes, small wooden camp cottages provided by plantation owners; others rushed to a nearby hotel, nicknamed the Hotel of Sorrows, to consummate their marriage. It is said that on those nights, from inside the wooden building, the soft sound of the brides' weeping could be heard, mixing with the mournful wails of ocean birds.

Why did the women weep?

Some cried from homesickness. They had left home, relatives and friends and might never return. Others sobbed because after an exhausting sea journey they had been too quickly bedded by their eager husbands.

Many a bride was confronted at the Honolulu docks by someone who looked nothing at all like the picture she had been pressing to her heart. Her new husband was older or homelier, poorer or uglier. She must spend the rest of her life with someone she was sure she would never love.

Most picture brides eventually adjusted to life in Hawai'i, loving their husbands, raising numerous children, caring for plantation homes and also working in the fields. These strong couples, merging lives in such a less-than-romantic way, raised children who became leaders in Hawai'i business, education and politics. 🌴

Hawai'i's beloved Lili'uokalani wed John Dominis ...

The queen has mother-in-law problems

John Dominis and the little girl who would become Queen Lili'uokalani first met when they were very young. She was playing in the yard of Royal School in Honolulu, the special boarding school for children of kings and chiefs, when she saw a *haole* (foreign) boy peering over the fence from the day school next door.

The royal children were objects of interest to everyone in the islands, and the *haole* boy shyly asked Lili'uokalani if she was a princess. Confused about her royal role, Lili'uokalani did not respond. She had been adopted by the royal family; she was not descended from the royal Kamehameha line, though her ancestors had been *ali'i* (chiefs).

As one of the youngest children at the Royal School, she greatly admired her *hānai* (adopted) sister Bernice Pauahi, who was several years older and mothered her. Whereas Pauahi was beautiful, quiet and bookish, Lili'uokalani was talkative, playful and loved music and dancing. Occasionally, she heard grownups discussing Hawai'i's political problems: the ever-growing dominance of ambitious *haole*.

Lili'uokalani knew foreign countries were jockeying to gain control of the beautiful islands, strategically placed in the center of the ocean. But it seemed to have little to do with the perky little girl. She was the youngest and there were many in line to rule Hawai'i, including her *hānai* brothers, Princes Alexander and Lot.

As they grew older, Lili'uokalani occasionally caught sight of John, the curious "boy next door." Tall, thin and handsome, he seemed a sensitive lad, and was very close to his widowed mother.

Lili'uokalani learned his family's sad story. John's father had been a trader. Leaving two older daughters in school in Boston, the Dominis' had come to the islands where John's father invested all of his money in his lifelong dream – a fine mansion in the center of Honolulu. He was on a journey to purchase furniture for the home when he was lost at sea. John's mother was left with a mansion, but no money, and so took in boarders to support herself and her son. John was a helpful lad, kind and attentive to his struggling mother.

By the time he and Lili'uokalani reached their late teens, John had become a friend and confidant of Prince Lot and so he was often in the company of the royal family. Their lives were full of fun: music, dances, *luau* and visits to the neighboring islands.

One day the king was returning to Honolulu accompanied by a cavalcade of about 200 riders, including John, who by then was a general. John was riding next to Lili'uokalani when a spooked horse came between them and he was thrown from his saddle. His leg badly broken, John was in great pain, but he gallantly insisted on accompanying Lili'uokalani home. At her door, he even dismounted to help her down from her horse.

When John had reached his own home, the leg was badly swollen and he had to be carried down from his horse. He was confined to his home for several weeks until the bones mended.

But what a dashing thing to do! Lili'uokalani was impressed when she learned what he had suffered on her account. Still, a few weeks later she became engaged to another man, Prince William, destined to one day be king. Lili'uokalani knew William was impetuous and had been courting another woman, Princess Victoria, so she at first declined his marriage proposal. He persisted and she finally agreed. However, Lili'uokalani and her family became more concerned about William's character and so she broke the engagement.

Shortly thereafter, John proposed and Lili'uokalani accepted. Soon, she began to realize how much Mrs. Dominis dominated her son. John knew his mother would not be pleased that he was marrying a Hawaiian, so he delayed telling her. Then, he put off introducing Lili'uokalani. When he finally did, the elderly lady was barely civil to her.

On September 16, 1862, in the home of Charles Reed and Bernice Pauahi Bishop, John and Liliʻuokalani were finally wed, three years after they had become engaged. His mother did not attend.

John took Liliʻuokalani to live at Washington Place, the palatial home his father had built, where his mother was still very much in charge. Years later, Liliʻuokalani wrote in her memoirs: "As she felt that no one should step between her and her child, naturally I, as her son's wife, was considered an intruder; and I was forced to realize this from the beginning...

"My husband was extremely kind and considerate of me, yet he would not swerve to the one side or to the other in any matter where there was danger of hurting his mother's feelings. I respected the closeness of the tie between mother and son, and conformed my own ideas, so far as I could, to encourage and assist my husband in his devotion to his mother."

Liliʻuokalani tried to please her mother-in-law by assuming small household jobs, but Mrs. Dominis seemed at first displeased with the marriage, then simply detached from it. Liliʻuokalani and John continued living at Washington Place, but Liliʻuokalani eventually secured a small beachfront estate at Waikīkī, where she spent much quiet time writing music and poetry. John often joined her there.

"Later in life," Liliʻuokalani wrote, "Mrs. Dominis seemed to fully realize that there had been some self-sacrifice, and she became more and more a tender and affectionate mother to me as her days were drawing to a close."

Liliʻuokalani's peace was short-lived. One after another of her royal relatives ascended the throne, only to die after short reigns. The many newcomers flooding the islands from around the world brought diseases for which the isolated Hawaiians had no resistance. Both royals and commoners succumbed to measles, typhoid, leprosy and even simple infections. There were at least 300,000 Hawaiians when the explorer Captain James Cook visited the islands in 1779. A hundred years later, there were fewer than 60,000. Lili'uokalani composed the sorrowful song *Aloha 'Oe* as an ode to her dying race.

It seemed sometimes as though the gods themselves wanted to destroy the Hawaiian monarchy. Mysteriously, few members of the royal family seemed able to bear children. Neither Pauahi nor Lili'uokalani became pregnant. And the two babies who were born to other relatives succumbed to illnesses.

By the time she was in her early 50s, her husband ill and his mother dead, Lili'uokalani would endure the greatest challenge of her life and the greatest sadness ever faced by Hawaiians. Her *hānai* brother, King David Kalākaua, died. Bernice Puahi refused to rule. So Lili'uokalani, the once-carefree youngest child who had had little training or desire to be queen, was to lead her people during the time of their greatest turmoil.

Prosperous businessmen and plantation owners, some of them descendants of the very missionaries who had come to save the islanders, wanted to secure their interests in the islands. As American warships stood in Honolulu harbor, the men coerced Lili'uokalani into signing a document that allowed them to take over the government. Queen Lili'uokalani, under duress, temporarily surrendered, sure that President Grover Cleveland, whom she had met and considered a friend, would rectify the situation and restore the monarchy. Although he sympathized with her cause, he did not.

Two years later, a few hundred of her subjects, loyal Hawaiians, plotted to regain the monarchy. They were unsuccessful and the queen, aware of the plan, was arrested and imprisoned for nine months in a room at 'Iolani Palace, once the scene of many happy times. There, she prayed and wrote her music, listening to her guards constantly pacing past her door.

After her release, Lili'uokalani retired, alone, to Washington Place. Today, the small mansion she shared with her husband and his beloved mother is the official home of Hawai'i's governors.

Lili'uokalani was devoted to her people and worked for their welfare. She was particularly concerned about the future of Hawaiian children and the education of Hawai'i's young women. To this day, her estate continues to fund good works through the Queen Lili'uokalani Children's Centers. 🌴

Ko'olau and his family fled to Kaua'i's mountains.

The leper's wife: no greater love

Pi'ilani, Kaleimanu, an unidentified woman and Ko'olau, the paniolo (cowboy) leper.

From about 1850 until the mid-1900s, dreaded Hansen's Disease, or leprosy, ravaged these islands, striking people of all nationalities, and taking a particularly deadly toll among Hawaiians and Asians. Although most patients survived for many years, it was usually assumed they would die, the disease eating away fingers, toes, face or limbs.

Children were examined for leprosy in schools; neighbors watched to see who showed the rash or sores that signaled onslaught of the disease. Bounties were offered for leprosy sufferers and suspected patients were captured, quarantined and banished for life to Kalaupapa on an isolated peninsula of Moloka'i. Living conditions were appalling for many years, until Father Joseph Damien DeVeuster came to the settlement in 1873 and began cultivating the land, building shelters and caring for patients and orphans.

41

In the 1860s, while he was still in his twenties, the Hawaiian *paniolo* (cowboy) Ko'olau and his two-year-old son Kaleimanu contracted leprosy. Ko'olau refused to be sent to Moloka'i because it would mean breaking up his family, leaving his lovely wife Pi'ilani behind. The family and several other lepers gathered up a few belongings and fled deep into Kaua'i's Kalalau Valley along the Nā Pali coast, hunted by armed government troops. Some stories say they were spotted by two soldiers, and to protect his family Ko'olau shot the soldiers. Others say the sheriff was so enthralled by Pi'ilani's beauty that he attempted to rape her and Ko'olau shot him during a struggle to protect her.

Whichever the case, Ko'olau, an intensely religious man, had become not just a fugitive leper, but a hunted murderer. Now there was no turning back for the little family. They fled deeper into the treacherous cliffs and valleys where few soldiers dared follow. Constantly on alert, forever fearing capture, moving from cave to tree, they eluded searchers as the days became months and the months became years.

The disease, unchecked and unmedicated, ate away at both father and son. But perhaps poor Pi'ilani suffered most, watching her dear family endure such pain. After three-and-a-half years of hiding, Ko'olau died. Pi'ilani buried her beloved husband in a secret place, which she never revealed. History records no further mention of her son Kaleimanu.

Leprosy extracted a great sacrifice from those who loved its victims. In later years, perhaps in part because of Ko'olau's tragic story, Kalaupapa patients could bring spouses with them to the settlement. For the spouse, that meant giving up personal freedom, sometimes permanently, and facing the possibility of contracting leprosy.

For some of the years, a patient or spouse who gave birth at Kalaupapa would be forbidden to touch the child. Parents could view the baby for a few hours or days through the window of a hospital ward, then the child was sent to live with relatives or adopted off island.

Not until 1959 was a cure found for leprosy. Kalaupapa's residents were free to leave. Many did go; others who had grown accustomed to life at the settlement stayed. Today, a handful of Hansen's Disease patients still live at the peninsula, which has been designated a national park. 🌴

He was on a velocipede; she tried not to laugh.

A missionary descendant *falls* in love

In the late 1800s, Frank Baldwin, a descendant of two Hawai'i missionary families, literally fell into his future wife's life from a bicycle. It was one of those massive velocipedes with a huge front wheel and a tiny back wheel, very dangerous and apt to change one's life remarkably.

Some missionary descendants, by virtue of being in the right place at the right time, inherited large land holdings, built businesses and amassed fortunes in the rapidly developing islands. Missionary children and their descendants were often sent to the United States for schooling.

In the late 1800s, the Baldwin family sent Frank, nicknamed "General" for his aggressive play on Maui's polo fields, to Oakland High School in California.

One day, Frank was cycling past Miss Horton's School for Girls in Oakland when a group of children began to pursue him. They were hitting the velocipede's back wheel, attempting to tip it over, and Frank was trying to escape. The velocipede toppled – a perilous situation considering its height.

Watching the handsome young man from the front lawn of Miss Horton's School was a pretty girl named Harriet Kittredge. Her father owned a thriving lumber business and the family ranked high on California's social ladder. Harriet and her sister Ethel had been presented at court in London, a rare honor, and had also "come out" socially in San Francisco. Naturally, her family had plans for Harriet to marry someone whom they knew and of whom they approved.

But then that velocipede tipped over – and so did the Kittredge's plans.

Harriet ran to help Frank. He was unhurt . . . but he was angry at the children who had overturned his cycle and he let them know it. In fact, he was so upset it was a few moments before he noticed Harriet, who was somewhat shocked at his outburst.

They looked into each other's eyes and Frank was calmed. The young couple talked for awhile and Harriet rather boldly invited him to a "dance evening" at her school.

Probably she giggled with her school chums about the meeting. Probably she bought a special gown for the affair and waited with beating heart. One thing is certain: Harriet's future had changed forever.

Frank went on to Yale, Harriet to nursing school; but soon they abandoned those endeavors and decided to wed and move to Frank's home-island, Maui, where he would help manage his family's businesses.

Harriet's family was wary about her decision. Harriet and her mother embarked on a visit to Frank's parents in the quiet Sandwich Islands, to get a clearer picture of the Baldwins and of what Harriet's life would be like. They found that the lives of wealthy islanders were simple, but filled with friends and special joys. Harriet and Frank wed in April, 1900, and moved permanently to the island of Maui where horses, not velocipedes, were a favorite means of travel.

The couple had four children, lived long happy lives and contributed greatly to life in the islands. 🌴

The island of O'ahu has its own Romeo and Juliet tale.

Kaaru and Kenichi are wed in heaven

BOB FIJAL PHOTOS

"We Shall Be United Again"

On the night of May 22, 1919, Uyeda Kaaru, 17, and Okimoto Kenichi, 18, sat on the beach holding each other close. Both cried softly. A few feet away, the waves kissed the sand. Above, stars blinked happily, unaware of Kaaru's and Kenichi's plight. Only the sad-faced moon seemed to share their sorrow. This was to be their last night together. Indeed, it would be their last night on earth.

Kaaru and Kenichi had grown up as neighbors in a little fishing village near Wai'anae on the island of O'ahu. Abandoned by her father, Kaaru had been adopted by a childless couple when she was six, after her own mother died. A gentle girl and a loving daughter, Kaaru as a young woman worked in the plantation fields and also took care of her invalid adopted mother. Kenichi, also a dutiful child, lived with his parents and labored at a nearby mill.

It was the custom among Japanese for the parents to select a spouse for their sons and daughters, sometimes without consulting the child. Kenichi's father followed this custom and, unknown to his son, he had chosen a girl from his home village in Japan as Kenichi's bride.

When Kaaru and Kenichi learned they could not wed, they were unconsolable. They sat on the beach all night and pondered their plight. They were bound by duty and parental obligations to fulfill their parents' demands; but they loved each other so much they could not spend their lives apart, married to others they did not love.

In Asian cultures, obeying parents and protecting the family name from dishonor are very important. At the same time, to die for a good cause is considered honorable. This is what the couple was raised to believe.

Finally, that night on the beach, they decided their only recourse was to be united in the afterlife. In a sense, theirs was to be a marriage made in heaven.

The next morning, May 23, 1919, Kaaru and Kenichi went to a little house near the beach. They wrote short farewell notes begging their parents' forgiveness and asking to be buried in the same grave. Kenichi poured some formaldehyde in a cup, gave Kaaru a drink, and then also swallowed from the cup. Each died a painful death a few hours later.

The double suicide caused shock and sadness throughout the islands. Kaaru and Kenichi were buried together as they had requested. To this day, on the anniversary of the couple's death, members of the Japanese-Hawaiian community burn incense at their grave in Wai'anae's Japanese cemetery. The grave is marked by a headstone with the words "We Shall Be United Again." 🌴

TONI POLANCY PHOTO

*She took a tapa cloth from
the wall and covered them. Thus,*

She married a prince

The first time Myrtle King saw Prince David Kaapuawaokamehameha he was standing in front of his home, a grass hut at Punalu'u on the windward side of the island of O'ahu, wearing only a red *malo*, a piece of cloth tied around his hips. A teacher at the rural village of Waialua in the 1930s, Myrtle had brought her students to meet the man known throughout the islands for retaining the Hawaiian way of life.

"When he came smiling to meet us, it was the first time I ever had a Hawaiian greet me with the beautiful word 'Aloha,' long dear to me," Myrtle wrote.

In their garden at Punalu'u on the rural windward side of O'ahu,
David Kaapu teaches his children – infant daughter Kapua
and son Kekoa – to pound poi. Mrytle holds Kapua.

"And the grass house! It seemed to me the most perfect dwelling a heart could desire when I stepped in with my bare feet upon its beautiful matted floor – a floor to sit and sleep and live on, not merely to walk on with shod feet."

Born in Oregon in 1898, daughter of a powerful politician, Myrtle had been a strong-minded child. Her mother called her "contrary."

"My mother found that the simplest way to get me to do something was to tell me particularly not to do that," Myrtle wrote.

During the 1920s, while most women were concerned with house-keeping and childbearing, Myrtle was a daring adventurer. By 1930, when she met King David, the descendant of Hawaiian *ali'i* (chiefs), she had already hitchhiked across the United States and journeyed throughout much of the world. Accompanied by equally heroic women friends, she'd camped, climbed, hiked and taught in Japan, China, Indochina and India.

Movies and airlines had brought the world to Hawai'i's doorstep; the islands were embarking on a commercial period of history that bastardized Polynesian culture. Hawaiians had become ashamed of their own customs and, in secluded parts of the islands, sometimes hid from tourists who might ridicule them.

Attempting to preserve some of the authentic history of his ancestors, David chose an unusual life style. On inherited lands, against the mystic backdrop of the Ko'olau Mountains in rural Punalu'u, he constructed an encampment of grass huts, exactly as they had been built by early Polynesians. Here, with few modern conveniences and wearing only the *malo*, or loincloth of a native, David lived simply, growing much of his food in a nearby taro patch and gardens.

Myrtle was immediately attracted to the golden-skinned man who exuded gentle wisdom. But it was not David's beauty and life style that most intrigued her.

"Some of the stories of his life that he told me last spring when I camped nearby with my school children were probably what finally convinced me that I had found in him all the qualities I most desire in a husband. The first is intelligence. It seemed to me I had found in this naked Hawaiian a more civilized mind . . . than I could often discover in my fellow white men."

Although he had little traditional schooling, David was a philosopher and a *kahuna* (teacher), sharing knowledge and the history of his people with tourists and visitors who stopped at his houses, including dignitaries such as President Roosevelt and movie star Shirley Temple.

"What is the secret of David's attraction for the most prominent visitors to the islands – and for me?" Myrtle asks. "I think it is due to two things for which nearly all American souls are hungry, because of their relative scarcity among us. I think it is, for one thing, because he is an artist, a true creative artist, using nature as his materials and putting art into his own living, his implements of life. We have had to take our art in galleries and museums where it failed to satisfy. Seeing it alive in the heart of a man and in the work of his hands, his houses, his garden, his clothing, his utensils, brings wistful looks into many faces and tears to some eyes."

David and Myrtle's friendship grew slowly over several years. Myrtle was planning a trip to another island when she boldly wrote David a letter:

Dearest David,

In case the plane should crack up or the Kauai boat sink, I want you to know that I love you, that I am hoping I can be your wife. I have loved you ever since I first saw you and talked with you...

David, if a spirit can stay near the loved one, I shall be your guardian angel, and every night you sleep in your grass house I shall be there in your arms where I longed to be, your very own.

If you can find a good wife I shall be happy. Only she must be real, like you, a genuine Hawaiian, and she must love the life you live, not take you from it.

Aloha pumehana

Ka Likolehua

Myrtle survived the journey to the island of Kaua'i and one evening upon her return, she and David were sitting together in his grass house. She arose, took a Hawaiian *tapa*, a bark cloth, from the wall and covered them.

"Do you know what this means?" David asked.

"Then I realized," Myrtle writes, "that yes, of course, I had several times heard him tell visitors that the Hawaiian wedding ceremony was simply to sleep together under the same *tapa*! So I agreed that I knew – and thus I had married us! It was a matter that needed no discussion; we both just knew that that was how it was meant to be."

David had found his true Hawaiian soulmate and she was a *haole*, foreign woman. A legal ceremony followed at the courthouse in Kāne'ohe, O'ahu.

The Kaapuawaokamehameha's marriage produced two children: a boy, Kekoa, and a girl, Kapua. The family lived for several years in the grass houses.

Myrtle wrote: "In our ensuing over thirty-six years of marriage if anyone asked how it came to pass, I would say, 'Oh, I just broke into the tightly locked-up place and captured the wild man!'

"To which he would add, 'Oh no! I *kahunaed* you!' In other words, he spirited me over from Waialua." 🌴

I Married a Prince, a Cinderella story from Hawai'i by Myrtle King Kaapu @ 1977 by Myrtle King Kaapu.

One of several authentic grass houses David built at Punaluʻu.
Each house had a function: preparing food, sleeping, dining, praying.

*The relationship between the world's richest woman
and Hawai'i's greatest athlete may have gone*

Beyond passion

Hawai'i has boasted queens and kings, princes and princesses, but two famous Dukes stand out in her romantic history. Doris Duke, in the 1940s, the richest woman in the world, and Duke Kahanamoku, Olympic athlete and father of modern surfing, shared a love of the ocean and an understanding of the price to be paid for fame: privacy.

It has been more than six decades since the two tall, handsome Dukes strolled across Oahu's beaches, yet their story is kept alive in books, movies and legend. How much of what is said of their relationship is fact, how much fiction? Only the two Dukes knew for sure and both of them are dead now. Yet one thing seems certain: their relationship transcended the purely sexual.

Their story begins in September 1935. Duke Kahanamoku, at 45, was an international swimming champion, having won medals in both the 1912 and 1920 Olympics, and was also a Hollywood movie actor and sheriff of Honolulu. He assigned himself the duty of guarding tobacco heiress Doris Duke, 23, and her first husband, politician James (Jimmy) Cromwell. The Cromwells arrived in the Hawaiian islands on the last leg of a long honeymoon that was not going well.

Doris' father had died when she was a child, admonishing her to "trust no one" and guard his fortune. On their wedding night the over-anxious Jimmy allegedly asked his new bride how much allowance she was going to give him and Doris quickly grew to suspect he had married her for her money. The couple lived mostly apart and eventually separated during the last three years of their eight-year marriage. Doris spent much of the time in an extravagant estate, Shangri-La, which she built on several acres at the foot of Diamond Head, bordered by the ocean she loved.

Even if she weren't the richest woman in the world, Doris would have attracted attention. She was 5 feet, 10 inches tall with long, shapely legs and a beautiful body and, in a day when bathing suits still tended toward one-piece modesty, she wore a bright yellow two-piece swimsuit on busy Waikiki beach. Duke Kahanamoku's younger brothers taught her various ocean sports; she excelled at surfing and outrigger canoeing, winning several competitions.

HAWAI'I STATE ARCHIVES

History, rumor and some of the several books on Doris Duke, say she became romantically involved first with Sam, Duke's brother, and then with the charismatic Kahanamoku himself. Their romance, it is said, continued intermittently for more than ten years. His nickname for her was *Lahi Lahi,* which translates as 'soft as the wind.' That must have been comforting to a young woman who was becoming known as tough, aloof and unapproachable.

Doris Duke's times with the Hawaiians were probably some of the most peaceful in a life marred with often-misplaced suspicion of people. One thing attracted Doris to Duke and other Hawaiians – they were usually unimpressed by material goods and she knew Duke was never after her for her money.

By most accounts, Doris had at least two other serious lovers, movie actor Errol Flynn and Conservative member of Parliament Alec Cunningham-Reid, and she twice became pregnant. The first child was miscarried or aborted in a hospital in 1939. She discovered she was pregnant again in the Spring of 1940 while she was embroiled in a divorce from Cromwell. The law in those days gave the husband custody of any child conceived during a marriage, whether or not he had sired it. The thought that Cromwell might gain access to her child and/or her wealth alllegedly worried Doris.

Whatever her reason, legend says that on July 11, 1940, Doris Duke decided that she had only one option in regard to her unborn babe. She would surf it away. She rode into the pounding waves, taking on the most challenging and strenuous of them, and continued to surf for several hours. When she came in, tired and exhausted, she collapsed and was rushed to Queens Hospital in Honolulu, where she gave birth to a premature baby girl. The infant lived just twenty-four hours, but something happened to Doris in that short time. She fell in love with the child, whom she named Arden.

It is also possible, of course, despite legend, books and movies on the subject, that Doris Duke simply took on more wave than she could handle and the miscarriage was an accident. That would explain why Arden's birth was to haunt Doris, sending the wealthiest woman in the world on a life-long search for simple peace and happiness.

One thing about the legend of the Two Dukes is sure. Their friendship and respect for each other endured. Duke Kahanamoku married Caucasian entertainer Nadine Anderson and Doris Duke gave them a generous token of friendship. Not a gift, exactly.

When Duke was single, he had rented a house at the foot of Diamond Head," Nadine recalls in *Memories of Duke: The Legend Comes to Life.* "Later, we bought a house (in the Diamond Head area of Oahu). Fortunately, Doris Duke helped us with an interest-free loan, as Duke had no money. Duke lived here the rest of his life. We paid back the loan by monthly payments as rent." 🌴

He was Japanese/American; she was German. They were enemies, weren't they?

Mitsuo's WW II souvenir

Anneliese when she and Mitsuo first met.

It was 1945. The modern world's most devastating war had just ended and, like thousands of other jubilant American GIs, Mitsuo Sakamoto was anxious to go home. His unit, part of the 522nd Field Artillery Battalion, Charlie Battery, was deep inside Germany when armistice was announced and now they awaited orders in a town called Donauworth.

There was not much to do in Donauworth – hurry up and wait – and one evening as Mitsuo strolled the main street, ravaged by American bombs, he noticed a beautiful young blond German girl. Small and petite, she was standing in her yard, her partially-destroyed house looming behind her, and she was talking with some older women.

"As I got closer," Mitsuo writes, "I saw her face and immediately thought to myself *that's the face I want for me*. I fell in love at first sight, but I also knew it was impossible for me to have her."

He was Japanese/American; she was German. He lived three continents away, in Hawai'i. Even if their two countries had not just fought a great war, their cultures were a world apart.

His company, Charlie Battery, was part of the 442nd Regimental Combat team, a proud and unique group. Second and third generation Japanese whose ancestors had emigrated to Hawai'i and the U.S. mainland, the men had been anxious to prove where their sympathies lay after the Japanese bombed Pearl Harbor, catapulting the United States into World War II. And in seven major European campaigns the 442nd had well-fulfilled its goal. "You fought," President Harry S. Truman would one day tell the brave *nisei*, "not only the enemy, you fought prejudice and you won."

But as he strolled Donauworth's main street, Mitsuo's greatest personal challenge lie ahead. He, a short, dark Japanese/American had fallen head over heels, love at first sight for a petite German girl. How could anyone feel such happy emotion when the horrors of war were everywhere? So many losses, so many young men on both sides of the conflict, killed. Devastated by the war, German civilians functioned in stunned horror. Whole villages were destroyed. Food and supplies were scarce. In his memoir, *My Best World War II Souvenir,* Mitsuo describes German prisoners cooking and eating out of cans, stripping dead horses of their flesh.

Even now the pretty girl was making it quite clear how she felt about American soldiers. Two Army buddies of Mitsuo's were standing by the fence, calling out to her, trying to get her attention, and she was ignoring them. Mitsuo, handsome and clever, thought for a moment. How could he stand out from the competition?

He had an idea. He approached some children playing a few houses away and asked the young lady's name.

"Anneliese!" the children answered. And one of the boys volunteered the information that she was "a good girl."

The other soldiers were still at the fence, trying to get the good girl's attention. Mitsuo stood about 20 feet away and called out loud and clear, "Anneliese!"

"Quickly she turned around and looked toward me with a surprised, shocked look. She had never seen me before and I had called her name. Everyone turned to look at me. The two soldiers asked how I knew her name.

Jokingly I said, 'Me and the blonde girl went to the same school together.' As I said that, I looked at Anneliese. She was smiling; she knew what we were saying."

Realizing they had been outwitted, the soldiers left and Mitsuo introduced himself to the German ladies, who asked many questions about Hawaii. Civilians were under a curfew and soon they had to go inside their houses. Anneliese's mother was not ready that evening to let a cheeky Japanese/Hawaiian into her home, but Mitsuo persevered. Each evening after she returned from work at a nearby farm, Anneliese sat under a tree in

Anneliese and Mitsuo stroll the streets of Donauworth during their courtship.

her yard. Each evening Mitsuo came to the fence and the couple chatted. Anneliese had learned English in her German school and each day that they visited, her English improved.

"After a week, Anneliese told me her mother said it was okay to come into the house," Mitsuo writes. "Boy! Was I happy! Now I can get to know about Anneliese and her family. I wanted to help them in any way I could."

Anneliese studied piano and each night Mitsuo listened as she played. Then he socialized with the family.

"She is a very smart girl and an obedient one," Mitsuo wrote. "Japanese would call that *oyakoko* (patience). Another fine characteristic of her that I came to cherish most is what the Japanese call *gaman* (suffer in silence).

"Here was the dream girl for me, but it seemed impossible to have her.

First, she was the only child; I knew they would never let her go so far away to a place like Hawai'i.

"Second, she was still very young, only 15 and a half. I loved her very much but I kept it inside of me all the time. I had great respect for her."

Items such as soap, toothpaste, cigarettes and coffee were nearly impossible for Germans to get. Food was rationed to a small piece of meat weekly for each family. One day, Mitsuo brought a large can of pineapples which Anneliese particularly enjoyed.

"Come with me to Hawai'i," Mitsuo teased. "There you can eat all the pineapples you want."

Anneliese just laughed.

The visits continued for five months; then Mitsuo learned his unit was being sent home. For the rest of his company, that was good news. For Mitsuo, so in love, it was heartbreaking. During their last evening together, he asked for a clipping of her blond hair to keep with him always, a souvenir of the woman he would forever love.

"Well, the time came to say the final *auf Wiedersehen* – goodbye. It was very, very hard to say anything," Mitsuo writes. "We just held each other tight and kissed. It was only our third kiss. Yes, I could count them, they were so few."

It was a long journey from Germany to the west coast of the United States – a troop ship, then several flights on small planes. By the time he reached Travis Air Base in California, Mitsuo had made up his mind: he would re-enlist in the service for three more years if he could be re-stationed in Germany. Most soldiers wanted to come home to the U.S., so the Army was happy to have a volunteer who wanted to be in Germany.

Unfortunately he was sent to Fort Lee, Virginia, then to Fort Dix, New Jersey, where his personnel records were lost. Mitsuo's adventures getting back to Germany rival Ulysses' journey in *The Odyssey*. Through daring, wit (and even a bribe or two), after several months he made his way back to Donauworth and Anneliese. And despite Army whims, he managed to stay nearby.

Among the lessons Mitsuo had gleaned in the Army was the fact that quartermasters units handle food and other supplies. Mitsuo decided that if he could get into the quartermasters unit in Germany, he could help

Anneliese's family. But in Munich he was assigned a gruesome task. German families were being turned out of their homes, their houses and furniture confiscated for the families of American soldiers. It was Mitsuo's job to guard the door of the homes as German families carried out what possessions they were allowed. He hated the work, so he tricked an officer into reassigning him.

"I told him I was hit in the head during the war," Mitsuo recalled in an interview for this book. "I said, 'Some days I go crazy. I hate these Germans.' I let him know he would be responsible if I attacked a German family."

Anneliese and Mitsuo on their wedding day. She had just one request for their wedding: a dozen yellow roses. Mitsuo found them.

"He said, 'I don't want you under my command. Get out of here today.' And he gave me a three-day pass." Mitsuo used the time and some connections to get himself assigned to the quartermasters unit.

Three years later, he was visiting Anneliese and her family regularly. By then she was 18 years old, nearing marriageable age. To be near her, he re-enlisted a second time, for another three years. Now, their courtship in the recovering Germany began in earnest, with dates to movies and bingo at the enlisted men's club.

"Some weekends I would drive Anneliese and her parents to a small farm village called Tussenhausen. Her mother was born there and she still had relatives farming in that little village. The farm life was hard work with long hours. I know about the farmer's kid's life, too. I grew up on a coffee farm.

"So, I would go to the PX and buy some chocolates and chewing gum. The kiddies' faces were all lit up when Anneliese's mother passed out those goodies."

In 1952, Mitsuo proposed.

"He said," Anneliese remembers, "'Make up your mind, because I won't re-enlist again. If I go you will never see me again.' And so then I realized I would miss him and I said I would marry him."

"Anneliese was a very caring person," Mitsuo wrote. "She always listened to her parents. But she had to listen to her heart, to do what her heart wanted. I knew that her parents loved her so much, no mattter how it hurt them, they wanted to see Anneliese happy,

"When Anneliese signed the marriage application, I made a silent promise to myself that she could go home anytime to visit her parents in Donauworth and stay as long as she wanted."

They began the long, arduous process of getting Army permission for an American soldier to marry a German woman. On October 28, 1952, after a patient seven years of longing for Anneliese and twice re-enlisting in the Army to be near her, Mitsuo married his most precious World War II souvenir.

The couple eventually made their way to Hawai'i, where their three daughters were born.

Mitsuo remained in the Army, retiring after 20 years. He was able to keep his two promises to Anneliese. She eats plenty of pineapple. And she has visited Germany 59 times in the years since their marriage. 🌴

'Umia ka hanu
Hold the breath
Be patient; don't give up

60

Lehua got what she prayed for...

Sometimes, you just know

In 1819, the missionary Hiram Bingham prayed for a spouse and his prayers were answered. In 1948, Lehua Lee Loy prayed for guidance. Her prayers were also answered – within hours.

At 23, Lehua had just graduated from beauty school on the mainland. It was Saturday afternoon. That evening she was scheduled to go out with a man she did not really care for and she was at odds with herself.

Strolling in downtown Honolulu, she stopped at the Cathedral of Our Lady of Peace to ask God to help her decide her next step in life. She wanted to marry, but had no real prospects. Yes, she had boyfriends, but no one she loved enough to marry. Should she return to her hometown, Hilo, and open a beauty shop? *Please God,* she prayed, *show me the way.* Then she genuflected before the altar and left the cathedral.

Reluctant to return home, she decided to take the first bus she saw and simply go for a ride. That bus, chosen at random, took her to a neighborhood where an acquaintance lived. Rose Martin, called Auntie Rose by everyone who knew her, was also from Hilo, and Lehua decided to stop and visit. Auntie Rose wasn't home, but soon a car pulled up. As Lehua watched from the porch, a handsome Hawaiian man helped Auntie Rose out of the car.

"Oh, cute!" Lehua thought. That was all; he left before Auntie Rose could introduce Herbert Weatherwax, newly returned from serving in World War II.

Meanwhile, Herbert, on his way home, felt restless. He just did not want to return to his apartment. Suddenly, for no reason that he could explain, he turned his car around and went back to Auntie Rose's house. As he pulled up, a pretty young woman was leaving. Auntie introduced them and they sat on the porch for a few minutes, talking. Eight years older than Lehua and also from Hilo, Herbert remembered her as a child. Totally charmed, he came right to the point.

"Are you married?" he asked Lehua. Straight out, just like that.

"No, I'm looking," she responded. Very honestly.

"I'm available," he answered. Quickly. Without thinking. But he meant it.

Herb knew how to court a good Catholic girl – the next morning, he took Lehua to Mass. They realized immediately that they were destined to marry, but Herb believed a man should own a house before he took on the responsibility of a wife and children, so they waited two years to wed. They bought a house in Kaneʻohe, Oʻahu, two weeks before the ceremony.

These days, Lehua's prayers have a different theme: *Mahalo* (thank you), *God, for 50 happy years, three good children and a forthright, loving husband. Oh yes, and for that bus ride.* ❦

He pili kau, he pili alo.
Close to the back, close to the front.
*The husband, standing in back of his wife as her protector;
the wife, the protected one.*

Portuguese immigrants to Hawai'i brought families – and a sensitive romantic custom.

Marry me, he sang

Unmarried Portuguese women were not allowed to date, but men could visit them at home during chaperoned sewing bees. Several young women would gather at a house where they stitched or crocheted busily while young men serenaded them, broaching the subject of love in song. Once a young man had chosen a bride he would stand outside her home, alone or with a few friends, playing guitar and singing. He might also send his beloved a sonnet or a love letter. If those first steps were well-received, he called on her parents to ask formally for permission to begin courting her. Because men greatly outnumbered women for many years in Hawai'i, a young woman often received several proposals. Portuguese women were more fortunate than those of some cultures – parents usually allowed their daughters to choose their own mates. 🌴

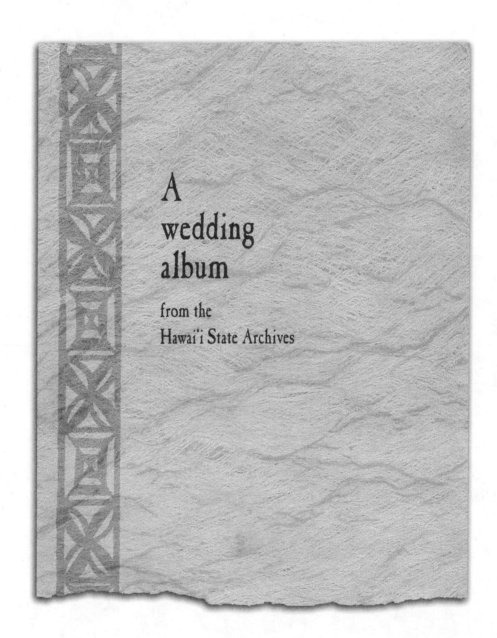

A
wedding
album

from the
Hawai'i State Archives

The Hawaii State Archives, storehouse for island history, is a small building behind 'Iolani Palace in downtown Honolulu. Among the records, books, and photos is a folder marked simply: Weddings. These pictures, most dateless and nameless, are the vestiges of society events, images captured in a camera's lens because the bride and groom were important or related to someone powerful in the islands. Above, the wedding party of Julia Judd and Mr. F.M. Swanzy in 1887. Julia was a descendent of Dr. Gerrit Judd, a physician and former American missionary who served as foreign affairs advisor to Kings Kamehameha III and IV in the 1840s. Opposite page, unidentified newlyweds, possibly Portuguese, and a little dog, pose carefully for a wedding photo.

Entering St. Andrew's Cathedral in downtown Honolulu is Miss Betty Lou Dillingham on the arm of her father Walter Dilllingham. Walter and Louise Dillingham were for many years Hawaii's "first family" socially. Their fortune was made in transportation and shipping.

The bride Betty Lou, her father Walter Dillingham, little Gail Dillingham and Mrs. Lowell Dillingham prepare to walk down the aisle.

Mr. and Mrs. William Chickering are married by Judge Walter F. Friar, former governor of the territory of Hawaii.

Mr. and Mrs. Edgar Reeve Bryant cut their elaborate wedding cake.
She is the former Miss Spayer.

Stanford University star fullback Bobby Grayson with his bride, the former Christine Williams.

Hiroshi and Hisako Sakamoto were wed at a Buddhist Temple on Maui in 1934. Nisei, or second generation Japanese, their parents had come to the islands to work in the plantations. They met when Hiroshi, door-to-door salesman for a drug store, visited Hisako's home at a plantation camp on Maui. Their two children, Roy and Charlotte, still live in Hawai'i.

Now

there is no place in the world
as amorous as Hawai'i. And it is not just
whispering kisses and rainbow encounters
that make our islands romantic. It is

Us. You and me . . .

All of us – god, goddess, princess, Polynesian, missionary, planter, picture bride, yesterday's visitor – have come to live together in this special, blessed place on tiny islands in the middle of an ocean, tossed together by fate, rocked by seas and time. Here, we each celebrate our own version of romance; we love deeply, ardently, intensely.

ALL OF THE FOLLOWING STORIES ARE TRUE, but some are more factual than others. Many subjects who shared their stories allowed us to use their names; others preferred to remain anonymous. When first names only are used in a story, the names are fictitious to protect the privacy of the subjects.

*Against odds of 150 million to one,
an old World War II photo is catalyst
for a modern Cinderella story.*

From Russia, comes love

It is a simple old photo taken at the end of World War II: two soldiers standing in stark contrast to each other – the thinner, darker man in the simple drab garb of an American soldier next to the heavier Russian officer, formal and distinguished in his coat and medals.

In the joyous pandemonium of the historic first meeting of Russian and American troops at Elbe River in Torgau, Germany, in April 1945, the two men posed together. The American was Herbert Weatherwax, 24, Hawaiian, from the island of O'ahu, a world away culturally and geographically. A draftee, he had survived the attack at Pearl Harbor. Trained as a signal corpsman, he and his outfit followed the famed 442nd Regimental Combat Team to France, where he cleared land mines for General George Patton's charging tank corps. The day the photo was taken there was a feeling of camaraderie, a sense that the war was over.

After the war, Herb returned to Hawai'i. Eventually, he met lovely Lehua Lee Loy, bought a home, married and raised three children. Life was busy and full, but occasionally – even during the Cold War between the Soviet Union and the United States – he would take out an old album and remember. He studied the photo of himself and that Russian officer, cherished souvenir of an historic time. He felt a kinship – here were two very different men from opposite sides of the world who had fought for the same cause, thrown together for an instant. Unlikely brothers frozen in time by the blink of a shutter.

Herb had already retired when in 1991 the opportunity arose to travel to Russia as part of a contingent of Americans starting a self-help organization there. He took the picture along. He wasn't really expecting or even hoping to find his soldier. After all, he didn't even know the man's name and there are 150 million people in the Soviet Union.

In Russia he passed the photo around every time he was in a gathering of even a few people. Always, it was the same. His hosts would look at the photo and shake their heads. "*Nyet. Nyet.*" No. No.

At a meeting in St. Petersburg, he passed the photo once. Nyet. Then, on a whim, he passed it around again. This time a beautiful redheaded woman, whom we will call Tanya for this story, stared at the photo.

"That looks like my father!" she whispered in amazement. "I will ask him," she promised Herb.

The next day she called. Yes, her father had been photographed with an American soldier at Torgau. Against impossible odds, Herbert had found his soldier and Leonid Kruglov was as happy as Herb to make the incredible connection. In fact, Leonid sent Herb a gift – the leather military pouch he had carried during World War II.

Touched by her father's gift, Herb told Tanya, a professor at a Soviet university, that if she ever visited the United States, she must come to Hawai'i. A year later, she called from Seattle, where she was taking part in an exchange program.

76

"Come to Hawai'i," Herb insisted. "You can stay with us." So Tanya came to Hawai'i to visit the family of a man her father had posed with for less than a minute 47 years before.

One night, Tanya was invited to a gathering in O'ahu. When she returned to the Weatherwax home that evening, she seemed somewhat excited. Herb's wife Lehua remembers it this way:

"Tell me. What means the word 'available?'" Tanya asked.

Lehua told Tanya, "If a man asked you, it means he would like to go out with you, to know you better. It means he likes you."

Tanya shook her head. *"Nyet. Nyet."*

"Somebody fell in love with you," Lehua teased.

"Impossible!" insisted Tanya.

"Who is this person?" Lehua asked

To the Weatherwaxes' amazement, Tanya named a well-known Hawai'i man from a prominent island family.

The next day, the gentleman called and asked Tanya to dinner. Eventually they were wed in a simple ceremony in Hawai'i.

As special as the day was for the wedded couple – it was perhaps even more so for two former soldiers who had posed together so many years before. Eventually Leonid Kruglov visited Hawai'i and resided with the Weatherwax family. He and Herb became good friends. They took another picture together, this time not as strangers but as friends whom fate had brought together despite a great distance, a Cold War, many years and staggering odds. Now the men, truly allies, shared more than a great war – having been catalysts for a unique love story, they were, in a sense, *ohana*, family. 🌴

78

Did Sharon dream this?
No, she insists,
it really happened.

A cave
and candlelight

Sharon was snuggled peacefully in her sleeping bag at Waiʻānapanapa beach, near Hana, Maui early one morning when she felt a series of light kisses on the back of her neck. She knew from the warm smell of shaving lotion that it was Ben. She inhaled deeply, savoring the scent mixed with the cool, salty ocean air and, finally, reluctantly, opened her eyes.

Overnight camping, making love in a sleeping bag, was a new experience for Sharon and she was surprised at how deeply she had slept; the waves whispering to the black sand a few feet away from her was a gentle, repetitive lullaby.

But why was Ben waking her now? Before the sun had even risen?

Another kiss, a gentle nibble on the tip of her ear. "Come on, sleepy head," he whispered, "I have a surprise for you!"

She smiled peacefully and snuggled deeper into the sleeping bag. "What?"

He kissed her temple and the top of her forehead. "You have to come with me. Follow me."

She frowned. She laughed. She opened her eyes reluctantly and reached for her jeans.

"No," he said. "It's okay. Just the way you are. Just put your sneakers on."

"You're crazy," she said. "Someone might see."

"There's no one here but us. I'll wrap you in this."

She stood up, naked and shivering, and he gently placed a *pareo* around her. Aiming his flashlight in their path with one hand and holding his other arm around her shoulders, he began to lead her up a small incline, over a few lava rocks. Suddenly Sharon saw a soft light shining from the side of a large lava flow.

She was fascinated. "What is that?" she whispered.

Ben smiled. "It's your surprise. Come closer."

Another 100 yards and Sharon began to discern a small cave. The inside of the cave glowed. As Ben led her into the cave, she realized the light came from dozens of candles he had placed inside. The flickering light made shadows dance on the walls.

She was awestruck. "It's so beautiful! You did this for me?"

Ben drew her toward him, held her close, and turned her to face the opening of the cave.

"From here, we'll watch the sunrise," he said.

After a few minutes, a soft pink glow filled the sky. Then something amazing happened. Just as the light from outside grew brighter, the candles near the opening of the cave began, one by one, to go out.

"Ohh!" Sharon murmured. "It's so lovely! As though someone were awakening the world, kissing the night away."

To this day, neither Sharon nor Ben know why the candles, of their own accord, went out. It is as if the *menehunes*, Hawai'i's forest elves, wanted to add their own magic to what was already a beautifully romantic experience, one that Sharon will remember all her life. ❋

E lei no au i ko aloha.
I will cherish your love as a beautiful adornment.

Suzie was dying of cancer. The animals were like medicine...

They save lives and vice versa

Suzie and Sylvan Schwab sleep with a goat in their bedroom. The goat wears diapers, which Suzie changes regularly. Occasionally, the Schwabs also share the sleeping quarters of their Ha'iku, Maui, home with litters of kittens and puppies, fawns, pigs and a bevy of birds.

The Schwabs operate the East Maui Animal Refuge and their story is unique.

Suzie and Sylvan met in Maui 22 years ago. From California, Suzie was visiting friends who lived in a beachfront condo next to Sylvan, a photographer.

"She was the girl next door," he says.

"On our first date," Suzie remembers, "Sylvan had this dog he kept petting. I'd never seen anyone spend so much time with a dog and I liked that. The next time he saw me, there was a bird nesting in my hair."

One night Sylvan told Suzie he loved her. She began to cry and ran down to the beach. Sylvan ran after her, caught her and held her close.

"What's wrong? Don't you love me?"

"Yes, I love you," she said. "But I don't want you to love me."

Suzie explained that she was suffering from terminal kidney cancer and had come to Maui to die, sparing her family the agony of caring for her.

Sylvan, very much in love, decided that rather than share Suzie's acceptance of death, he would do everything he could to save her. He began taking her three times a week to a Chinese doctor, Jon Young, in Honolulu. Young treated Suzie with a combination of diet and acupuncture, but advised that she needed more. She needed a positive reason to get up every day, a reason to live.

Sylvan was aware of Suzie's strong love for animals. Every time they visited a pet store, she cuddled ill or injured animals. He began collecting animals for her. Bird breeders and pet shops contributed ill or deformed animals they couldn't sell.

"Suzie was supposed to be dying of kidney cancer. The animals were like pills to keep her alive," he says. "Whenever we brought another animal home, she perked up. She had a purpose to live, to help keep these animals alive."

After a year of treatment, and many animal rescues, doctors proclaimed Suzie cured, all traces of her cancer gone. The Schwabs eventually married – at the Maui zoo – and decided to dedicate their lives to the creatures that had helped save Suzie. If they could do anything about it, no animal they could reach would die from neglect.

The Schwabs soon began reaching a lot of animals from a variety of sources. Breeders and pet shops donated less-than-perfect pets. State forestry officials brought orphaned, sick or injured birds, including some fallen from nests. Families contributed pets they couldn't care for, such as ducks purchased at Easter. The Maui Humane Society turned over birds and animals they were not equipped to handle. Hunters brought in babies who'd survived their mother's slaughter, like the piglet found in its mother's belly.

Over the 20 years since they began their "Boo Boo Zoo", the Schwabs have housed thousands of animals, as many as 400 at a time, including a lamb with a thyroid condition; cats suffering from skin cancer in the tropical sun; kittens blinded by a bacterial infection; a one-legged love bird, victim of a rat attack; a cockatoo with a rare form of AIDS; a dog found at the airport with razor slashes and cigarette burns on his face; a neurotic parrot who picks at itself nervously, and a three-legged goat who lives in a sling suspended from a ceiling and receives daily physical therapy.

Today, the Schwabs live on two acres in Ha'iku, Maui, in a compound designed for animals. Several corrals and pens hold the large, active animals. The first floor of their house is devoted to smaller animals and birds. They reside on the second and third floors, amid animals like the diapered goat who needs special attention.

Animals arrive at the shelter covered with ticks, fleas and lice, and the Schwabs spend hours cleaning them. Sometimes, Suzie has mouths to feed every ten minutes of every hour, night and day. In between, she must wash and dry up to 12 loads of bedding. Sylvan awakens each morning to man a shovel and hose, keeping the compound clear of animal excrement.

The "Boo Boo Zoo" is licensed by the state and federal governments to care for injured birds, but receives no government funds. A veterinarian donates his services and several volunteers help cuddle and clean the animals, but the Schwabs use their own funds and rely on tax deductible donations to pay over $150,000 in annual bills for food, medicine and supplies.

Animals are occasionally adopted by qualified "parents", but some – like goats, hogs and deer – cannot be returned to nature and will spend the rest of their lives

happily roaming the little compound. (Goats, hogs and deer endanger Hawai'i's fragile ecosystem by gobbling up plants.)

The Schwabs eventually learned that Suzie suffers from lupus, an immune system disease about which little is known. The same loving care that helped her overcome cancer is keeping her active and happy.

"I've broken an arm before, but no one wanted to shoot me!" Suzie says. "I mean, when you go to the emergency room I hope to God the doctors don't decide it might cost too much to care for you." 🌴

*"There's nothing illegal about marrying someone
you are committed to, about loving someone
and not having sex."* •

The village secret

Christina talks about her ex-husband and her face lights up with joy.
"I love Jimmy," she says, breathlessly. "I will always love Jimmy."

When they met some 15 years ago, Jimmy, then 31, was a gregarious
waiter at a restaurant in a rural village. Christina, just 20, was a carefree

bus girl. He had lived on the islands all his life; she had come recently from
another country.

Christina loved the village and the villagers who had immediately accepted
her. She felt she had found a cozy corner in which to live the rest of her life.

Jimmy, small and blonde, was everyone's buddy, Christina says. "He was the guy who made everyone's work experience a good one – joking, rubbing tired shoulders.

"He was, he still is, the happiest person I've ever met. No blinders on. He's just out there living his life and singing. Trusting and loving everybody."

Each night before work began, the employees formed a circle, held hands and prayed briefly together. Christina had a secret she prayed no one would discover. She was an illegal alien with no green card that would allow her to work and remain in the islands.

One day after she had been working at the restaurant for several weeks, her boss asked for Christina's green card. She was devastated; she wanted to spend her life in that little village community. She shared her plight with her co-workers and when Jimmy heard, he volunteered to marry her.

Christina knew Jimmy was gay and had long been in a serious, stable relationship, so their marriage would be one solely of necessity. Once married, she could remain in the United States forever if she so chose. They did not discuss how long the marriage would last or when they would part.

One day on a beach in a little bay, with several friends present, Jimmy and Christina were wed. Stephen, Jimmy's longtime partner, was best man. Stephen supplied the ring, a golden one he had once found while digging in the garden.

Christina insists the marriage was no sham – that she and Jimmy truly loved each other and always will.

"During the ceremony he was looking me in the eyes. He said he would honor and respect me all my life and I repeated the same thing."

The threesome went to live in the men's small house. There, Stephen cooked and kept house and worked on several projects; Christina and Jimmy remained at the restaurant. Stephen and Jimmy slept in one bedroom; Christina in another. Although the marriage was never consummated, it was a happy one.

"I used to tell people, 'I am the happiest married woman I know.'"

Her eyes grow soft, her voice wistful.

"We had many good conversations during those years. We shared some of the important parts of life, awakening the spiritual part of me. I could tell Jimmy anything, share anything, the deepest thoughts. He helped me grow up."

Jimmy and Stephen had always been open about their relationship. Now, villagers occasionally teased Christina about the marriage. "Hey, where's your husband, Christina? How your marriage going?"

It was, she says, a kind of secret kept by the entire village and she loved her co-workers and the villagers for knowing and accepting her unique lifestyle.

After they had been married for awhile, Christina began a relationship with another man, Bob. For several months, the four of them lived together – happily, she says.

Now, villagers teased her. "Hey Christina, your husband he know you are cheating on him?"

The marriage lasted for five years and might have gone on forever, but eventually Jimmy and Stephen started a successful business. By law, if anything happened to Jimmy, Christina would inherit. By mutual consent, Christina and Jimmy divorced.

"They needed me to divorce them," Christina jokes.

Although she has had several relationships in the ten years since her marriage, Christina has remained single. Finding the qualities Jimmy had, establishing a relationship like theirs, is difficult.

"The men you like, you can't talk to; the men you enjoy, you don't like," she says.

She is still friends with Jimmy and Stephen, still lives in the same village, though in separate houses.

"We are family and will always be. I know one thing: there's nothing illegal about marrying someone you are committed to, about marrying someone and loving someone and not having sex. We may not have had sex, but we did love each other and that bond is stronger than many heterosexual marriages."

Every person looking for love should have a pet like...

Baby, the flirting dog

Laura, a hotel concierge, moved to the islands a few years ago with her boyfriend, Dave. Both were dog-lovers, and soon after renting an apartment that allowed pets, they adopted a cuddly female puppy from the local humane society. They enjoyed the mixed Shepherd pup, training her, playing with her and naming her their "Baby."

Within a year after their arrival on the islands, Laura and Dave separated. Laura weathered the break-up pretty well... but Baby didn't. Baby whined at the door when it was time for Dave to return home and seemed listless, missing the good times she'd had rough-housing with him. There are psychiatrists, social workers and self-help sessions to assist children with the trauma of separation, but no such aid for pets.

Laura comforted Baby as best she could and eventually the dog seemed better. But as time wore on, Laura became aware of a strange pattern. Every time she took Baby to the beach, the dog sought out a solitary male and laid down next to him. Laura, of course, would run over and retrieve her.

"I'm so sorry! " she would say.

And soon Laura learned that Baby's bad habit, which continues to this day, is a kind of blessing. It is a very reliable way to meet men.

"The guy's reaction to Baby not only breaks the ice, it tells me a lot about him. If he laughs and is warm toward the dog, well… I'd probably like him," Laura says.

If the man looks interesting and has no woman friend in sight, Laura will pull Baby off the blanket and say, "I'm so sorry!" Then she may add, strictly as explanation, of course, "My boyfriend and I broke up a few months ago and every time we come to the beach the dog embarrasses me like this!"

Often, the conversation continues from there. Baby's penchant for meeting men has gleaned Laura several dates and a few long-term friendships.

"I haven't met a serious boyfriend yet, but I know I will eventually. Baby is very determined to find a daddy." 🌴

Cheating? Don't let the fish see

Early Polynesian life was rich with omens. Fishermen, gone from home for days at a time, seemed especially susceptible to fishy portents. Imagine a lonely fisherman gazing into the ocean. He sees *uhu* (parrot fish) darting about playfully and worries that his wife is also darting about, making whoopee and failing to observe the fishing *kapu* which decrees solemnity be maintained at home while he is away. Or he notes two *uhu* rubbing noses and suspects something fishy is happening at home.

Worse yet, as he's fishing the unfortunate husband might suddenly break a hook. He is certain that his wife is having sex with another man. Anxious and irate, he heads for home.

Considering the numerous omens and a fisherman's obsession with his wife's loyalty, it's a wonder many fish were caught. Then again, perhaps the omens were a ruse, a trick to keep the clever *uhu* from becoming a main course. 🌴

*Without exchanging a word,
within a few minutes,
he would decide if
he wanted to marry her.*

The faceless
fiancé

Shawna and her family were cutting sugar cane in the field of their small Fiji plantation when she heard a car coming up the street. She threw down her machete and ran to the house to make herself ready.

Automobiles were rare in rural Fiji, even in 1993. Whenever Shawna or her sisters heard one approaching, they knew it was a prospective husband coming to look at them.

The man who was coming to see her was named Basavaraj and he was 33 years old. His aunt was Shawna's neighbor. Born in Fiji, he had gone to work in Hawai'i six years before. Now, his parents had decided Basavaraj needed a wife and they insisted he return to Fiji to find one. Basavaraj, on a two-week vacation from his job, looked at the woman his parents had chosen for him and rejected her. Then, since time was limited, he had quickly visited several other prospective brides and rejected them all.

Now Basavaraj, obviously not easily satisfied, was coming to see Shawna.

In many Indian families, even those whose ancestors migrated to Fiji years ago, tradition still dictates much of life. Parents choose mates for their children. If they approve a match, the would-be groom comes calling at the prospective

MATTHEW THAYER PHOTO

bride's home. With her relatives present, the woman serves tea and the couple looks at each other, sometimes, as in Shawna's case, for the first time.

Tradition decrees they must not speak to each other, so without exchanging a word, within a few minutes, Basavaraj would decide if he wanted to marry Shawna. If he did, custom says she has one opportunity, without ever having spoken to him, to decide whether she will accept the proposal. So Shawna was understandably nervous.

She had lived all her life on the small plantation in Fiji and at 20 she was already considered a bit of an old maid. Several men had come to view pretty, petite Shawna and had chosen her as wife, but she had rejected them all. She had a dream that kept her from marrying: she wanted to travel and see the world outside her little island, to live a life more eventful than that of her brothers and sisters, most of whom were already raising families.

If her appearance and demeanor appealed to Basavaraj, he might fulfill the dream she had carried since childhood. Shawna uncoiled thick dark hair that fell to her waist and shook her head, letting the hair spring loose and around her heart-shaped face. Then, she donned the traditional *sari* and went to meet her fate.

Talkative when she was with friends, Shawna was shy around strangers. The traditional tea ceremony is a graceful rite, designed to show off the prospective bride's beauty and polish. But when she served the tea, Shawna's hands shook so hard the dishes clattered on the tray.

Basavaraj took the cup she offered and neither spoke a word. He was looking at her, she knew; and by custom she was allowed to look at him, but she was so nervous she could not bring herself to raise her head and see his face, not even once.

She breathed in relief when the short ceremony was over; she had performed poorly and was embarrassed. This successful man who worked in sophisticated Hawai'i would not want such a clumsy country girl for a wife, but at least the ordeal was finished.

A few minutes later Shawna went to change from her sari into clothing more appropriate for her life on a plantation, but as she passed the windows she noticed Basavaraj was still on the *lāna'i*, the wide porch. She heard the low murmur of voices. That could mean he had chosen her, that he and her brothers were negotiating her marriage.

Oh dear! She should have seen him. She should have looked at the man who might sit across the dining table from her for the rest of her life, glimpsed the face that might loom over her in the marriage bed. Did he have kind eyes? Was he handsome? Was he ugly?

Shawna crept to the window and peeked out, but all she could see was a blurry profile.

Soon one of her brothers came into the house.

"He wants to marry you. Will you marry him?"

"Yes." She said. Sight unseen. Nature unknown. She wanted to go to Hawai'i. Her brother went out onto the *lāna'i* and gave Basavaraj the good news. And, according to custom, he left without ever having said a word to Shawna. He would not see her again until their wedding day.

Only a few more days remained before Basavaraj would return to Hawai'i, so preparations for the marriage were rushed. He had visited her house on Friday. On Saturday Shawna and her sisters made a wedding bower of wood and decorated it with fresh flowers. On Monday, under this bower, she and Basavaraj drank from the same cup in front of family and friends in their wedding ceremony.

As he lifted the cup to her lips, Shawna looked into Basavaraj's face for the first time. It was a long, dark, handsome face. As her lips touched the wedding cup, his eyes met hers, and they were gentle, intelligent eyes. Here was a good man to lead her across an ocean to a new life.

Today, Basavaraj, Shawna and their two young daughters live happily in a condominium in a busy Hawai'i town. They love and respect each other.

Tradition, Shawna says, chose wisely. 🌴

Someone was poking and tickling her.
She thought it was Daryl.

Menage a trois, Maui style

Daryl, a longtime Maui bachelor, tells this story about one of the best first dates he ever had. He and a new woman friend went snorkeling at Molokini crater near the southern tip of Maui.

The couple hardly knew each other and conversation was a bit stilted. Eyes closed, dressed in a skimpy bikini suit, she reclined on a float in the water next to the boat, rocked gently by the waves just a few yards from where Daryl sat. He watched longingly, wanting to say something to move the relationship forward, wishing he had the nerve to tell her how scrumptious she looked.

Suddenly she began giggling. "Hey, cut it out! Stop tickling me!" She laughed, swatting the water playfully.

Something was poking and tickling her. She thought Daryl had dived under the float and was being playful. He hadn't. And a few seconds later, they were both surprised to see a dolphin peering up at them. The friendly mammal had been playfully nudging her from under the float with his nose. Soon Daryl and his date were laughing together like old friends.

"That crazy dolphin did what I didn't have the nerve to do," Daryl chuckles. "He made the first move and it really broke the ice. I knew just how far I could go without getting her mad – and it was a lot farther than I thought!"

Some *kama'aina*, Hawai'i longtimers, put a mystical spin to the story. Dolphins, they say, are so tuned in to people that they can read our minds. The helpful dolphin in this story, they insist, had sensed Daryl's longing and was simply lending a hand or, in this case, a nose. 🌴

*The first year
of their relationship
Mitzi and Joey
could not even
discuss religion.*

Having faith in each other

She is Roman Catholic; he is Buddhist. And when they began dating three years ago, concerned friends and family members warned Mitzi Kraensel and Joey Toro that they should not consider marriage.

Cross-cultural marriages are common in Hawai'i, but Buddhism and Catholicism are very different. Catholics pray to God, sometimes petitioning his emissaries, Mary and the saints, to intervene on their behalf. Buddhists believe that life is not preordained, and that the ability to lead a life of value and spiritual fulfillment derives from within, through methods such as chanting, study and meditation.

It would be easier, some friends said, if religion meant less to Mitzi and Joey, but both are extremely devout. Mitzi, 26, is a Eucharistic minister, dispensing communion at Sunday Mass. She attended Catholic schools and once wanted to become a nun. Joey, 31, is youth counselor for his temple, where his family is very active.

Indeed, their faiths are so different that the first year of their relationship Mitzi and Joey could not even discuss religion without arguing.

Religion aside, Mitzi, a *haole*, or foreigner, and Joey, of Filipino and

Puerto Rican descent, seem an unlikely pair. Mitzi moved to the islands several years ago; Joey's family has lived on Maui for five generations. Their romance blossomed very slowly at a video store where Mitzi worked while attending college. Attracted by her giddy humor and her "sunflower brown" eyes, Joey would come in almost daily to rent videos and to chat.

Mitzi liked his seriousness and how much he seemed to care about the youth at his temple.

"I thought, 'He is solid. He has the right values to be a good boyfriend,'" Mitzi remembers.

After several months of waiting for Joey to ask her out, Mitzi took the initiative. She suggested he join her and "some friends" who were going dancing. On the scheduled day she called to tell him the friends had bowed out, hoping he would finally ask for a date. He did.

Over the next few weeks, they became inseparable, hiking through bamboo forests to secluded waterfalls, strolling on moonlit beaches, dressing up for weekly dinner and movie dates.

Mitzi's eyes were happy when she looked into Joey's; his were gentle and protecting. As they sat in her parents' living room, their bodies were never far apart, their hands rested softly in each other's, her parents realized the couple was in love, even before they did. And reaction to the relationship was guarded.

"Our first reaction when we met Joey was that this is a very nice young man but he is Buddhist," SallyAnn Kraensel, Mitzi's mother, recalls. "Our family tries to live our Catholic beliefs, not just talk about them. The Catholic and Buddhist doctrines are very different."

The first tentative year of their relationship, Joey and Mitzi existed in a kind of soft and trusting glow, sure that their love was stronger than any obstacles. They avoided the topic of religion when they were alone together. The few times the subject came up, arguments ensued.

So, ignoring the issue that stood between them like a simmering volcano, Mitzi and Joey simply enjoyed each other and quietly let their love for each other grow. His parents were calmly optimistic.

"We were well aware of their differences," Joey's parents said, "but knew these differences would not stop them from being happy as long as they worked at it. We are a cross-cultural couple ourselves and know the difficulties, but overcoming these difficulties as they arise makes the relationship stronger.

"(Mitzi's religion) is not important to us. The fact that she is a good person and that she makes Joey happy is what is important."

A year after their first date, they finally began to address religious issues, each learning more about the other's faith. Mitzi accompanied Joey on some of the outings with the youth of his temple.

After they had been together three years, Joey decided they should wed. Like a scene in a Hollywood movie, he got down on one knee in the middle of their favorite restaurant and, to the joy of restaurant patrons, he produced a ring and proposed marriage. A sobbing, trembling, very surprised Mitzi quickly said yes.

Now the topic they had skirted through three years of courtship had to be faced. Her faith called for Mitzi to be wed in a Catholic Church. The Buddhist rite is also full of tradition and ritual, including a wedding chant and a San San Kudo, a wine or sake ceremony.

What kind of wedding should they have? And where?

Before those questions had to be answered, Mitzi's faith dictated the next step. Catholics who plan to wed must attend "engaged encounters," a series of classes and lectures designed to introduce them to family life within their faith. Joey and Mitzi attended a weekend-long retreat on Kaua'i.

"They asked hard questions," Mitzi says, "and made us answer them.

"Who's going to take care of the bills?

"How many children do you want to have?

"What do you expect from each other in marriage?"

Surprisingly, there was little about religion in the weekend, Mitzi says. "It focused on the similarities in religions, not the differences.

"After all," she adds, "Our values are similar... and that's what attracted me to Joey originally."

They came away from the weekend having made real decisions about the future.

"Instead of making the children choose, we will all go together as a family to both religions," Mitzi adds. "The children will attend Catholic school. For after-school activities, they will go to Buddhist youth group."

The children will also attend Catholic high schools, she says, but will choose college: "Catholic or Buddhist or anywhere they want."

After much concern and prayer and discussing the issue with a priest, Mitzi's family is joyfully hopeful. "We know God will honor this marriage," her mother says. "I love the way Joey rolls his eyes when Mitzi says something off the wall, which is quite often. I love the protecting way he is around her. I love the way he loves my daughter."

Three years after they began dating, Mitzi and Joey were married in two ceremonies: first, an exchange of vows at a Catholic Church with both a priest and a Buddhist minister participating; then, a full Buddhist ceremony, including a 20-minute chant, at a hotel on the beach in Maui. The nuptials were followed by a seven-hour-long celebration with 400 guests which was taped for a nationally-syndicated television show.

Today, Mr. and Mrs. Joseph George Toro, Jr. still gaze into each other's eyes and see there a lifetime of happiness, made richer, they believe, by their very different faiths. 🌴

About 20,000 people marry in Hawai'i every year. Half are visitors; the rest are kama'aina, *residents, celebrating in ways unique to these islands.*

Mabuhay! Emily and Rufino are wed

One by one four men rose from long tables that filled the Lahaina, Maui, Community Center, raised glasses of champagne and saluted newlyweds Emily Maniago and Rufino Villanueva:

"*Mabuhay!*" "*Okole maluna!*" "*Banzai!*" "Cheers!"

The 800 guests at the Villanueva wedding toasted the second generation Filipino couple according to modern Hawaiian tradition – in Filipino, Hawaiian, Japanese and English, representing the guests' ethnic diversity.

Emily's religious heritage is Jehovah's Witness; Rufino's Roman Catholic. At their wedding in the garden of an oceanfront resort, a minister of Polynesian heritage performed a non-denominational ceremony.

Loreto, one of Rufino's six siblings, prepared food for the reception which lasted five hours. It included traditional Hawaiian *luau* food such as *kalua* pig and *haupia*, a coconut pudding.

Family and friends contributed hours of entertainment to the wedding reception. Emily's brother performed a traditional Tongan slap dance, his friend a Polynesian fire dance. A nephew, from Moloka'i, sang a solemn Hawaiian chant. Her three sisters performed a *hula*. According to Hawaiian tradition, the new husband sits in a chair as his wife dances a wedding *hula* in front of him. Since Emily was too busy to learn the dance, Leilani, a family friend, performed the wedding *hula* in front of guests.

Altogether Emily and Rufino's wedding and reception blended at least six cultures. And formed a culture of its own: *Hawai'i hou.* New Hawaiian. 🌴

*Lovers sometimes have
an adventuresome attitude that leads to...*

Passion in precarious places

In the movie *From Here to Eternity*, Deborah Kerr and Burt Lancaster rolled romantically on an O'ahu beach, waves threatening to wash them out to sea. Countless couples have copulated in tropical jungles, despite the mosquitoes. And it is simple island courtesy to ignore honeymooners hugging behind rocks, trysting in tall grass, or making love behind the darkened windows of stretch limousines.

But perhaps the riskiest place for a sexual encounter was one shared by Sandra and David.

After enjoying a romantic dinner, intimate conversation and warm sake at a fine restaurant, Susan and David emerged into the fragrant night air and felt a strong and immediate desire to express their affection. Across the dark road they noticed a big old tree with wide, low branches that were easy to climb upon.

The restaurant was busy, people were entering and exiting, but the tree's thick foliage prevented their seeing the copulating couple.

The precariousness of the situation added to the excitement, Susan says, and she and David will always cherish their encounter in the cradling limbs of that tree. 🌴

*20 years and 100 pounds later,
would he still want her?*

A weighty secret

As the Hawaiian Airlines' jet left the Honolulu airport and began its climb into the cloud-tufted skies toward Maui, Rosemary Widener felt her heart both sink in fear and leap for joy. She looked down at the endless blue water below and whispered, half to herself.

"I'm so excited. And I'm so terrified."

The woman next to her, a stranger, glanced at her. "What?"

"Oh, I didn't mean to bother you," Rosemary said. "I'm so excited. I'm about to meet a man I haven't seen for 20 years. And we may decide to marry."

The young woman turned to Rosemary. "How romantic!"

"Romantic?" Rosemary looked thoughtful. "Not as romantic as it sounds. I've grown older, I've gained about a hundred pounds in those years and he doesn't know it. I'm afraid he's going to be shocked."

The plane took on speed and Rosemary explained.

"Gary and I first knew each other many years ago. I worked for a computer company in Seattle and he was a salesman who called on us occasionally. We had coffee and dinner several times over a few months. Then one day he announced that he had been offered a job in Hawai'i – and he was moving. He suggested that I consider joining him there.

"I was tempted. I liked him a lot. But I had three children and a good job to support them. You can't just go off when your life is safe and set."

The woman looked thoughtful and shrugged, "I suppose so... "

"We communicated for several months and he urged me to come. One day I received a letter from him. He was getting married. And my life went on.

"That was more than 20 years ago. Then, six months ago I received another letter from Gary. After a long fight with cancer, his wife had died, he was lonesome and thinking of me. The letter delighted me, but frightened me too. I knew instinctively that if Gary and I resumed our relationship, it would be permanent. It's like you have something happen in your life that isn't finished and it has to be completed.

"We began to correspond again. Every Friday was date night. We'd play music, drink wine and talk on the phone. And of course, pretty soon he was again urging me to come to Hawai'i for a visit. But..."

"But you'd gained all that weight," her co-passenger finished.

"Yes! I was excited until I looked in the mirror and realized what those 20 years had done to me. Gary was picturing the 155-pound woman he had known, not the 277-pound woman I had become."

"But didn't you tell him?"

"No." Rosemary shook her head. "I should have, but I couldn't quite bring myself to do that. You know, I wouldn't even tell my kids or my friends how much I weighed. Gary and I exchanged pictures, but just our faces."

"But surely he has changed too!" the young girl said.

"Oh yes, of course. He's gray-haired now. But look," Rosemary reached into her blouse pocket and gently extracted a small photo. "Look. Here he is. See how his eyes shine? So full of life and laughter, just like 20 years ago.

"I told Gary I would visit him eventually. Then, I changed my diet, joined a fitness club, took aerobics and weight classes. I had tried those things before and failed. But now, with Gary waiting, it was much easier. I lost 60 pounds."

"Wow! Girl, you have a lot to be proud of," the young woman cheered.

"I suppose so, but I'm so scared. I'm still so overweight. Will he take one look at me and run away? Will I see disappointment on his face?"

The plane glided across a verdant valley patchworked with sugar cane and pineapple and shuddered onto the tarmac. Rosemary and her co-passenger exchanged a look like two schoolgirls about to peek at each other's test papers. The young woman patted Rosemary's knee. "You'll be fine. You'll see."

It seemed to Rosemary that the passengers took forever to collect their carry-ons and exit the plane. Yet, halfway through the walkway, she felt an urge to turn around and go back. Her co-passenger nudged her gently.

"You've come this far. Don't chicken out!"

The light inside the airport seemed blinding. All those people, staring at arriving passengers, grinning in anticipation. Rosemary scanned each face. Would she even recognize Gary? Would he recognize her? Or had he fled?

Then she saw him walking toward her, holding a *lei* in each hand. Gary was beaming, emanating a joy that matched hers.

"Here I am," Rosemary said. She searched his eyes. "Are you disappointed?"

He shook his head. "No, not at all." He placed the fragrant *lei* around her neck and kissed her. It was a kiss for which she had waited 20 years.

Behind them, Rosemary's co-passenger smiled and went on her way. 🌴

Life is wet and wonderful

Some couples marry and then begin to fight. Not Jack and Sissy Aaron. Their love blossomed during a battle filmed for the television show, *Magnum P.I.*

"There was this underwater fight scene. She was one of the bad guys," Jack remembers. Well known on the islands for his diving skills, Jack was underwater coordinator for the long-running series, starring actor Tom Selleck. He trained Selleck and several other cast members for under-water dives, but the first script called for a deep-water fight bet-ween a man and a woman, requiring considerable exper-ience. Jack quickly thought of a perfect double for actress Ina Balin. She was a beautiful woman he had known most of his life. As teenagers growing up in Kailua on O'ahu's windward shore, they had been romantically interested in each other.

"There were sparks," Jack says.
"Definitely sparks," Sissy agrees.

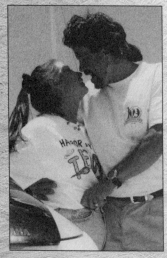

After high school, their lives had taken different paths and Sissy moved to Seattle. A few years ago, they met again at an island wedding. Sparks, never totally doused even in all that water, flamed anew. Jack quickly made five trips to Seattle and before long Sissy was back in the islands. The years since *Magnum P.I.* have been interesting for Jack, who owns Aaron's Dive Shop in Kailua. He's worked on nearly every movie or television show filmed in Hawai'i, including *Wind On The Water* with Bo Derek, *One West Waikiki* with Cheryl Ladd, *Baywatch* with David Hasselhoff, *War and Remembrance*, *Godzilla*, *Jake and the Fat Man* and *Pearl Harbor*.

Sissy, just as daring as Jack, recently drove a motor boat over two water skiers for a television commercial. She often doubles for the stars in underwater scenes and occasionally acts. 🌴

Women sometimes complain that professional men are difficult to come by in playful Hawai'i.

Prescription for love

Sherry wasn't at the singles bar looking for a husband, or even for a date. At 28, she just liked to dance and socialize. The bartender gave her a whiskey and soda by mistake and, on a lark, she looked for someone to give it to. She spied three clean-cut young men nearby, boldly walked up and offered the drink to the most handsome guy.

They introduced themselves – his name was Wes – and, inevitably, they began to discuss careers.

Wes asked what she did for a living.

"I'm a pharmacist," Sherry answered. "I work at (a large market)."

He laughed. "Really?"

"Yes, really. Why? What do you do?"

He hesitated, glancing over at one of his friends. "Well, I deliver the newspaper."

PAC Medical Clinic
Pacific Branch
5000 Front Street
Ph: 555-1212

North Branch
2400 N.W. 12th Avenue
Ph: 555-2424

FOR *Sherry*

ADDRESS: *123 LOVELY LANE, MAUI, HI* DATE *WORLD SERVICE*

℞ *HEAVENLY CHOCOLATE CONFECTIONS*

DISP: *ONE DOSE PACK – 1.8 Kg.*

SIG: *T-TI PO PIN FOR PLEASURE*

Wes Beale DPM
WES SMITH, DPM

BNDD NO.

☐ MAY SUBSTITUTE EQUIVALENT GENERIC

☒ X REFILL *AS MANY AS NECESSARY*

Her face must have fallen, because his buddies laughed and patted him on the back.

"Really?" She said. "I would have guessed you were…"

"Why? What's wrong with delivering newspapers?"

"Oh, nothing. But you seem…"

His buddies were grinning.

"I seem what?"

"You seem…" She shrugged, "Not like a delivery man. That's all."

"How do delivery men seem?"

"Oh, I don't know. You're teasing me now. I think it's fine that you deliver newspapers. As long as you like what you are doing, that's fine."

They chatted some more and danced a few times. Sherry appreciated Wes's wit and thought he seemed sophisticated and well-mannered. She really did not mind that his job was menial; after all, she was not looking for a serious relationship. But the evening was soon over and he had made no moves to see her again. She was a bit disappointed as she left the club.

Throughout the next day as she de-coded prescriptions and counted pills into little vials, Sherry occasionally thought of Wes.

Near quitting time, she glanced up at the clock and then over the high counter that separated her from customers. Standing in line was a well-dressed man wearing trousers and the expensive aloha shirt that marks a Hawai'i professional. The man was clutching a big bouquet of flowers and a large box of chocolates. It was Wes.

When his turn came, without a word, with just a smile, he handed her a prescription. It was from a local medical group. And his name was imprinted at the top: Dr. Wesley Beale.

The "prescription" instructed her to take "heavenly chocolate…for pleasure." In the area where a date should have been Wes had marked "date would be nice." He indicated the prescription could be refilled "as many times as necessary."

"You're a doctor?" Sherry laughed.

"I'm a doctor. Not that it matters, of course."

"Not in the least. But why didn't you tell me?"

"When you said you were a pharmacist," Wes explained, "it all fit so perfectly with my being a doctor that it was just kind of funny."

Of course Sherry filled and refilled Wes' pleasurable prescription. And to this day, she grins whenever she thinks of their first meeting. 🌴

There were few formalities to...

Faleone's proposal

The first morning in her new home Eileen awoke to a thud at the front door, followed by a voice. "Missus. Missus. You home?"

"Who...?" She squirmed out of bed and, wrapping on a *pareo* or sarong, went to the door. Leaving the brass chain attached, she opened it a crack and peered out. A brown-skinned man wearing baggy jeans and a simple shirt stood on the stoop.

"Yes?"

He stared at her for a long moment; his eyes very dark. Then he smiled, nodded, and pointed to her front yard.

"I come cut."

"Thanks," Eileen smiled faintly. "But I've already mowed the lawn."

"No, missus. No grass. Come. I show."

Moving quickly down the short driveway, he beckoned to her. After considering for a moment, she opened the screen door and followed.

Five tall coconut trees graced the narrow front yard; she squinted against the sun to see their tops. The man was pointing to the tallest one. Hanging like huge wooden ornaments was a cluster of coconuts.

"Coconuts ripe. Fall. Hurt. I cut for you."

Eileen groaned. Her two daughters grown, she had retired and moved to Hawai'i a few months before. Finding this sprawling old home with a reasonable price tag had been a godsend. While the house was in escrow, Eileen had cleaned and painted, mowed and pulled, washed, weeded and winced in pain.

Now here was still another major chore to be done – one she could not do herself.

"How much?" she asked.

"Forty dollars for one tree," he responded resolutely.

"Oh, I can't afford that," she exclaimed. "I'll pay fifteen."

He frowned, put his hands on his hips and studied the trees.

"Big trees," he said gruffly. "Thirty dollars."

"Twenty."

"I do $25. That all. No more talk."

"OK," Eileen said, "It's a deal."

"Deal." He shook her hand and smiled slightly. The palm felt hard, the skin stiff.

The next morning Eileen awoke to clacking, metallic sounds followed by loud thumps. From her bedroom window, she saw the small front yard covered by three-foot-long fronds. Her visitor from the previous day was swaying from the top of the tallest tree. A second man hacked at another tree, while a third man, heavyset, threw fronds into the back of a shiny blue truck.

On the ground, barely out of harm's way, sat two women in dark-colored long dresses; one held a baby. Eileen remembered hearing that immigrant families from Fiji, Samoa and Tonga resided in small communes and often labored en masse like this, everyone in the family helping.

"What are you going to do with those coconuts?" Eileen called out to the women. They smiled back, but said nothing.

"Ripe. We eat," the heavyset man responded. "You come here. You see. You have also!"

In a few minutes, Eileen sat cross-legged on the ground with the family, drinking fresh coconut milk. The men made a show of hacking the top of the coconuts neatly off with one blow of the machete and passing the fruits filled with sweet, blurry liquid.

106

The man who had come to her door shimmied effortlessly down the tallest tree. He nodded to her, put the coconut to his lips, threw back his head and drank deeply. Without his loose shirt, he looked slender, sinewy from the hard work. The muscles of his throat moved, sweat glistened on his brow. He had tied a cloth around it, just above his dark eyes.

The heavyset man was talking. "We are from Tonga. Now we live there." He nodded and pointed across the street. "Next road. Back of house there." So, they were her neighbors, their back yard visible from her front yard.

During the next few months, Eileen occasionally saw the Tongans' blue truck rumbling by. Whoever was in it — a flash of dark skin, a bright smile — honked, a quick short blast, and she waved.

A few months later, there was another thud on Eileen's door. The coconut trimmer. The palms needed trimming again, he said. She was busy working, but she stopped long enough to negotiate time and price. He turned to go and then quickly returned. "I have question."

"What?" Eileen asked. "I'm on the phone."

"I see no man. You marry?"

The question was so personal it stunned Eileen, but she was too busy to give the answer much thought.

"No," she said.

"I am not too," the man said. He departed quickly.

She was in her backyard early that evening when she heard a voice calling. "Missus. Missus."

It was the tree cutter. He was dressed oddly in a skirt that reached just below his knees. He wore a simple clean white shirt and around his waist a wide sash woven of leaves tied with a belt of coconut fiber. It must be his formal wear, she thought, he must be on his way to somewhere important. But why was he at her gate?

"Missus, I want come in. I give my name and village," he said.

Strange, maybe he wanted her to call him when the trees needed cutting. To be polite — he was a neighbor, after all — she opened the gate and got a piece of paper and a pencil. He sat down at a table on her *lāna'i* and began to laboriously print his name. Letter by letter, like a child. Before he had finished, he put the pencil down resolutely and looked up at her.

"I am Faleone. I am 47. I am divorced. And I have seven children!"

Eileen was puzzled. "Why are you telling me this?"

"And I will marry you."

Her first reaction was laughter. Her first words, "Oh, no!"

She should have been flattered, but she was simply stunned.

"I am 57," she said. "Too old for you."

He looked very earnest. "No. I have think," he said. "I am watch you. It be okay." He tried to take her hand but she moved it away.

"No! I'm sorry. That's impossible. Why don't you marry a Tongan woman? Someone from your village?"

None were available, he said. Custom, he explained, ruled that everyone should have a mate. Since she had none and he had none, marriage between them was possible.

"No, I have a boyfriend," she lied. "No."

He glanced toward the house. "I don't see man around. I am watch you. No man." Now she grew a bit fearful.

"He's away. He works off island. He'll be back soon. Now, you go!"

Faleone did not move. "It has been long since I have woman," he said sadly. "Too long. So long is bad."

"I can't help that. Please just go."

Still, he did not move. He held up one finger.

"One night?" he asked. "We have one night make love? One night only."

Now she was insulted. "No! You go! Now!"

"I go." He rose slowly and moved casually toward the gate. Nonchalantly, so that it could not be said he lost face; quickly enough so that it was not a challenge to her. Halfway, he paused and nodded toward a guava tree, its pungent yellow fruit littering the ground.

"Mess," he said. "I come cut. Just $200." He grinned.

She smiled. "$100," she said. 🌴

Kaua e tirohia te pai aahua,
engri te raupaa ko te ringa.

Take no heed of good looks, but rather of the callused hand.

Old Maori saying: Choose a husband for his work, not his appearance

108

*They both worked hard
and exercised at 4:30 a.m.*

The early bird
gets the governor

The early bird, they say, gets the worm. In Hawai'i, she also gets the governor. Vicki Liu, 40, was working out at 4:30 a.m. at the cushy Honolulu Club in 1995 when she spotted a familiar face also working out at that unlikely hour, Ben Cayetano, 56.

The couple had much in common: they were exercising early because each led a busy life. The mother of two children, then ages 9 and 12, Vicki was president and chief executive officer of one of the state's largest laundry services. Ben, who has three adult children, was governor of Hawaii, a very full-time occupation.

Vicki had been divorced from her first husband, a financial consultant, in 1992 after a ten-year marriage. Ben was recently divorced from his childhood sweetheart after a five-year separation.

Vicki described their first meeting for the *Star-Bulletin* newspaper:

"(Ben) walked up to me and said, 'Hello.'"

"I thought to myself, 'Oh gee, I'm sweaty. No makeup. I look like a wreck.' I just said hello to him. We started chatting. From that chat, things just went from there."

Their first date, lunch at the Hawai'i Prince Hotel, followed. Vicki surprised Ben by turning the tables on tradition. She presented him with a bouquet of spring flowers.

"He was so embarrassed, so I thought, 'Oh, oh, I don't think he's ever had a woman bring him flowers on a date.' He just stared at it. He didn't know what to do with it."

He got over the surprise and on May 5, 1997, they were married in a simple ceremony at the governor's mansion in downtown Honolulu. 🌴

The little glass dish

Years hence, decades from now, Summer Hansen Spaulding will pick up a little glass container, peer at the crystals of black sand it holds, close her eyes, smile and remember. She'll think back to one moonlit evening many years before when she and Ted Spaulding visited Hawai'i.

They had just finished dinner in a fancy restaurant and were enjoying a moonlit ride when Ted parked the car on a deserted road. Together they strolled onto a glimmering beach, its black sand crystals reflecting the moonlight.

Suddenly, Ted said. "Summer, turn around."

She gasped in surprise. Ted was kneeling in the traditional proposal pose, one knee making a deep impression in the sand.

"Summer, I would love for you to be my wife," he said.

She stood still, speechless.

"Well, answer me," he smiled. "Don't you want to marry me?"

"You didn't ask me a question," she teased.

So, still kneeling in that sand, Ted asked her.

"Summer Hansen, will you marry me?"

She said yes. *Yes, of course.* They hugged and kissed and, holding hands, walked and talked along that beach, planning a life together.

Then Summer went to the car, found a small plastic container and returned to the beach. This time, it was she who knelt – right there, where Ted's knee had made a round indentation in the sand. She carefully scooped up the black grains and took them home with her to Portland, Oregon.

There, in a glass container the precious black sand sits on a living room shelf. Summer occasionally takes the dish in her hand, caresses it, and remembers that very special night.

Someday years from now a child may ask – and later, maybe, a grandchild – about the little glass bowl. And Summer will tell its story. 🌴

If Cupid fails once, or even twice,
he's game to try again.

Cupid referees a match

Mike Sullivan's reddish hair was a bit tousled and his boyishly handsome face still a little flushed from push-ups as he sauntered across the market parking lot, packed with cars. Safeway was the largest – and busiest – market in the bustling seaside resort town of Lahaina. *Oh well, go with the flow*, Mike told himself. Born and raised on Maui, where his parents had migrated from Oregon many years before, Mike had absorbed the easy-going attitude of the islands. No rush. Talk story.

He was still several yards from the market when he glimpsed an attractive young woman just darting in. She had shoulder-length brown hair, a healthy tan and long legs that ended in Mike's favorite footgear: sneakers. Her short white skirt said she took her tennis seriously.

Wow, what a wholesome-looking girl, Mike noted. It was a fleeting bit of appreciation any bachelor in his twenties might experience, nothing more.

A few minutes later, Mike was stacking frozen television dinners in his grocery cart when he suddenly had a strange feeling, as though someone were watching. He looked up and the pretty young woman from the parking lot was standing a few feet away, gazing at him.

"Hello!" Mike smiled.

The girl snapped out of her reverie, gasped in embarrassment for having been caught staring and ducked behind a potato chip display. By the time Mike wheeled his cart over to find her, she was gone.

Wow! he thought. She is just gorgeous.

And he noted something else: her eyes were very bloodshot. *Booze? Drugs? Maybe she was not as wholesome as she appeared. Pity.* Then he moved over to the Perrier water and forgot about her.

Soon, Mike was standing in a long line at the checkout counter and – surprise! – the girl was right behind him. She was searching in her purse, pretending she hadn't noticed he was in front of her. Her long brown hair, delicately curled at the ends, swung softly over her face.

"Well, hello, there!" Mike almost bellowed. "What's your name?"

"Suzanne," she beamed at him. "Suzanne Iselin."

Soon Mike was thanking heaven for those long supermarket lines. Conversation came easily and by the time Mike reached the cash register, he and Suzanne had gleaned an amazing amount of information about each other. Her eyes were red and sore because as a tennis professional at Kapalua, one of the island's largest resorts, she had been teaching all afternoon in the intense sun.

And she had been staring at him, but she wasn't sure why. Somehow he seemed familiar. They soon realized the reason: the similarities in their lives were remarkable.

Both Suzanne and Mike had attended the University of Oregon at the same time, majoring in the same subject. In fact, her best friend at college was his resident advisor. Yet, scrambled among U of O's thousands of students, they could not remember ever having met.

Too soon, it was time for Mike to check out. As he left, he was thinking, *what a bubbly, endearing girl.*

And as Suzanne fumbled through checkout, her mind was racing. She wanted to know Mike better. But by the time she reached the parking lot, he was gone. Oh well, Suzanne figured, she'd probably never see him again.

She was wrong.

One of Suzanne's tennis students was dating a handsome man named Patrick. For several weeks she had been urging Suzanne to meet Patrick's brother. They were, she assured Suzanne, a perfect match.

Suzanne had reluctantly agreed to a date, but for various reasons it never took place. Secretly, Suzanne had been glad. She'd never been comfortable with blind dates.

The next time her student began urging, Suzanne had a new way of saying no.

"Too late!" she teased. "I've already met the man of my dreams." She described the supermarket encounter.

"Well, okay," the student shrugged, "but Mike is an awfully nice guy and you'd have so much in common."

"Mike?" Suzanne asked.

"Yes. Mike Sullivan. "

Suzanne was floored. The man she had been reluctant to date was the same man she longed to know better, the man she'd met in the market.

Meanwhile, his brother John called Mike. "Hey, I heard you were hitting on the tennis pro from Kapalua." John and his friends had seen Suzanne and Mike talking at the market.

"She's a really nice girl," Mike admitted. "Really nice."

The very next day, Mike called Suzanne. This time she didn't hesitate. She invited him to the resort for a tennis lesson. Coffee and lots of conversation followed.

They liked each other immediately, but each was already involved romantically with a person on the mainland. So, over the next three months, their relationship progressed more as friendship than romance. They became, Mike says, "buddies" – playing tennis, hiking, hanging out together.

Occasionally, Mike, half teasing, tried to kiss Suzanne. She'd laugh and duck away.

Soon, he decided the relationship had been on hold long enough. He travelled to the mainland and, without telling Suzanne, broke off the relationship with his long-time girlfriend. Then he invited Suzanne on a trip he knew she could not resist: a hike along the steep and mysterious Nā Pali coast on the island of Kaua'i. Tucked in his knapsack was something no one but he knew about: an engagement ring.

Nine years later, Mike and Suzanne have two children and are building a home in the foothills of the West Maui Mountains. They still go grocery shopping every week, together. And unlike the rest of us, they never grumble when the checkout lines are long. 🌴

John knows a joyful secret, thanks to

Kisses from heaven

After the police and the coroner left, John sat very still on the couch in the middle of the living room. He didn't cry, but for the first time in the 85 mostly happy years of his life, he didn't care if he lived or died.

They had just carried off the body of his wife Linda. John and Linda had been married for 63 years and sweethearts for 65. For the past 15 years she had been suffering from Alzheimer's Disease, slowly losing her memory and speech. John had cared for her as best he could, constructing various pieces of apparatus to offset Linda's failing abilities. For the last six years, he had nursed her night and day, feeding her baby food and intently watching her tiny face for signs of an occasional quivering smile.

Now, Linda was dead. As John sat alone in the living room, his mind shuffled through happy memories. The first time he'd seen her was at a college dance. He was a senior, she a freshman, radiant with sparkling eyes and dimpled cheeks. He couldn't take his eyes off her. Even now he remembered what it was like to touch her the first time they danced, to put his arm around her slender waist, to feel her soft hands in his. There followed many dates, dances. college functions, quiet walks through parks, hand in hand.

They married during the Great Depression. John landed a teaching position and Linda became head librarian in their California town. They raised two fine children and life was good.

Early in their relationship, Linda formed a playful habit she had continued for many years. When she wanted to make love, she would caress John gently in her own special pattern. She would come up behind him as he sat on the couch, lightly kiss him first on the tip of his nose, then on the tip of his ear and finally, soft as a feather, her lips would touch the top of his head.

Through the years they had occasionally vacationed in Hawai'i, and when it was time to retire, John and Linda moved to the islands. For awhile, they taught snorkeling to visitors. He could still see Linda in her gear, laughing behind the funny mask, a joy to be with.

They had taken their wedding vows seriously. He loved her, simply and fully, in sickness and in health, until death do us part. No, John thought as he looked at Linda's picture on the living room bookshelf. Not until death do us part. Even longer. Forever.

Suddenly, as he sat there remembering, John felt something touch his nose again and again, every so lightly. It annoyed him and with his hand he brushed it away. He saw from the corner of his eye something that appeared to be a fly, but larger and lighter. It moved to the tip of his ear and, annoyed, he again brushed it away. Then it softly touched the top of his bald head.

John leaped up – in recognition. Could the creature be his dear wife in the form of a tiny winged angel? As soon as this thought occurred to him, the creature disappeared, never to return. Yet John's heart was filled with joy.

Linda, after so many years of illness, had managed to signal her love to John. She was saying "I am here, waiting for you. Someday, we will be together."

And by her kisses Linda revealed to John a wonderful secret. In heaven, we are young again. We are reborn, playful and ready for love. 🌴

'Ale mai ke aloha kau i ka maka.
Love comes like a billow and rests before the eyes.

Said of an overwhelming love that leaves a constant yearning, with the image of one's affections ever present.

The case for love

TONI POLANCY

Sometimes the most unlikely objects unwittingly play cupid. A lawsuit over defective pipe brought Karen Lei Noland and Gary Gates together.

Maui's wastewater system had a problem: pipe, made of glue and fiberglass, was disintegrating and had become the subject of a lawsuit between the county and its manufacturer. Gary, a paralegal, was sent from California to Maui as part of a legal team in the suit.

On Maui, a friend invited Gary to a family gathering. "There," Gary says, "I laid eyes on one of the most beautiful women I've ever seen." Her name was Karen Lei Noland. Raised in Kentucky, Karen retained a slightly southern accent yet looked very Hawaiian. Of Chinese/Caucasian/Hawaiian lineage, her ancestors had been in the islands for generations and she was truly *kama 'aina* (of the land).

Gary found himself thinking of Karen often. He liked her outgoing manner, her friendliness. A few months later Karen again came to Maui for a family celebration. This time, Karen and Gary spent several hours talking, but she lived on O 'ahu and Gary was on Maui . "It never occurred to me to fly over to date her. Now I know that people here do that all the time," he says.

It would be nearly two years before Karen moved to Maui and the couple finally began a relationship. A few years later, they were wed. 🌺

Photos
by
Will
Spence

118

A *kama'aina* wedding

Karen Lei Noland's family has been in Hawai'i for generations so her wedding to Gary Gates at historic Leawala'i Congregational Church at Makena, Maui, was a true island affair. The reception included hula dancers swaying in the light of Chinese lanterns, a Hawaiian band, a falsetto singer and plenty of *lei*, the traditional gift of love. Bridesmaids presented long, green *maile lei* to groomsmen as they walked down the church aisle. And Karen and Gary also gave *lei* of thanks to all who had helped make their celebration a success.

120

Resources
for
romance

Create your own
island intrigue

Several women of various ages remember

Romantic moments

♥ I was sleeping and something sweet tickled my mouth. He was drizzling papaya juice on my lip. So gentle.

♥ He called me into the bedroom. It was glowing. He had Christmas lights strung across the top of a four-poster bed.

♥ He wore a leather explorer's hat into the shower. Water was dribbling down off it onto my body.

♥ He was a wonderful imitator. Once, while we made love, he pretended to be Jimmy Stewart. He kept murmuring with that voice and I couldn't stop laughing, until I stopped laughing.

♥ We made love under a waterfall. Just a little waterfall. Water splashing everywhere and I thought we'd drown.

♥ He just kept blowing gently all over me. I was lying on my back and he started at the back of my neck and it was as though he were casting a spell over me. I was so relaxed.

So, it is

spontaneity, creativity

that excite passion.

Will your love last?

Does your lover share the great affection you feel?
Is your spouse true and faithful?
'Ilima flowers can help you know the truth.

Fill a large cup with water. Pick two 'ilima flowers and set them side by side in the water. If the flowers float together, clinging to each other, your love is true and the relationship will last. If they drift apart, so will you and your lover.

TONI POLANCY PHOTOS

123

Hana aloha – magic spells

Ancients had a truly sweet way of securing the affection of those they desired. They used various types of sugar cane or flowers to cast love spells.

In the original versions of these spells, a *kahuna* or priest first prayed over the sugar cane or flower, dedicating it to Makanikeoe, a god of love. *Kahuna* still practice in some parts of Hawai'i, but if you cannot find one, you may meditate on the object of your desire and perform the rite yourself.

1. Holding a piece of sugar cane, meditate deeply for several minutes. Picture the person you desire and dwell on his or her beauty and personality traits. Then eat the cane and blow in his or her direction. The wind god Makanikeoe will carry the *mana* (power) to your beloved and he or she will soon be pining with desire, unable to eat or sleep until you have made love together.

2. After meditating, hold a flower and stand with your back to the wind. As the object of your desire passes, spit upon the flower, drop it, and say, "Spit! You come seeking me of your own accord!" If all goes well, when your beloved passes, he or she will be overcome with passion for you.

Or at least awfully curious about what it is you're doing. 🌴

Tricia Tupinio folds a crane.

1001 Cranes

In Japan, the crane symbolizes health. Giving an *origami* (folded paper) crane to a friend to wish "get well" or good health has long been a tradition. The Japanese who emigrated to Hawai'i brought the tradition here and then expanded it to hatch a completely new custom. Here, a bride displays 1001 origami cranes at her wedding reception, 1000 of which she has folded herself. The last one is folded by the groom.

Some brides spend as many as six months laboriously sculpting 1,000 little birds, usually of gold-colored paper. The birds are then hung from tree branches, bamboo poles or simply strung on cord and displayed at the wedding reception. They symbolize the bride's patience and perseverance, qualities that will serve her well, it is said, in marriage.

For many years, the birds were displayed and then unceremoniously saved in a sack, or worse, thrown away – all that work in the garbage heap. These days, the birds are sometimes used to form a picture or, if the family is Asian, to recreate the family's *mon*, or family crest, then framed and displayed, says Cathy Lancaster of O'ahu who designed the picture above. The beautifully preserved cranes become a family heirloom, a loving tribute both to a bride's tenacity and to a unique Hawai'i custom.

Men, know your flowers

Tammy Gallarde demonstrates.

It's oh-so-island to see *wahine* (women) wearing *pua* (flowers) in their hair. But *kane* (men), take heed! Look carefully. A *pua*-wearing *wahine* is sending you a message – and you'll need to be *akamai* (wise) to pick up on it. If the *wahine* wears *pua* over her left ear, she's telling you she's *kapu* (forbidden). She already has a *ku'u ipo* (my sweetheart) in her life. Stay away or at least be ready to put up with a little competition. If, however, she's wearing a flower on the right ear, she's telling you she's available and may be *aikane* (friendly), interested in meeting a *kane*. Approach her cautiously, carefully. A big smile helps. Talk story – slow, easy conversation, first. The *pua* gives you more than a clue – it gives you an opening. Try a first line like, "That's a beautiful flower. What kind is it?" or "Where did you get it?" Or, if you are *miala* (bold), consider, "That flower is almost as beautiful as you. But not quite." 🌴

Pick a way to show your love

Flowers are a symbol of love in many cultures, but Hawai'i's abundant flowers and liberal attitude toward picking them mean plenty of opportunities to express love in this fragrant and pretty way.

As you walk with your lover, pull a plumeria from a tree. Slowly pluck the individual petals and for each recite a reason why you love him.

MATTHEW THAYER PHOTO

Leave a different flower on her pillow or nightstand each night for a week, especially the week leading to the anniversary of your meeting. Attach a note or a bit of poetry you both enjoy.

Bestow upon her a bush of exotically scented nightblooming jasmine or gardenia, or a seedling from your favorite fragrant tree, perhaps a plumeria. Bring a spade and plant the gift in her garden or near her door to remind her of you. Then help her water and care for the plant, thereby nurturing your love. If she has no garden, buy a large potted plant for her *lānai* or living room.

Walk with your love along a secluded beach,
but first compose a delightful surprise – a
large, loving message written in the sand.

128

A present, given for no reason, exhibits your love.
But how much better to send eleven.

Gifts from the 'aina

The idea of sending multiple gifts has long been considered romantic and is meant to signify an enduring love.

When Mitzi Kraensel and Joey Toros were dating, she was full of loving surprises. She placed a huge sign proclaiming her affection alongside a highway where he was sure to see it on his way home from work. She spent the day decorating the Haiku Community Center and setting a fancy table with catered food. Then she took Joey there to dine, just the two of them, by candlelight.

But Mitzi's greatest surprise was one that lasted all day. She sent Joey eleven red roses, each delivered individually to him at work by a relative or friend. At quitting time, Mitzi delivered the last rose – a white one – herself.

Trashy beaches, loving treasures

If the object of your desire lives in Hawai'i, nature is your retailer and her merchandise is free. You can "shop" at the beach and in forests, choosing delicate natural gifts that are truly Hawaiian.

To find objects for the natural gifts below, hunt out beaches on the windward sides of the islands. These windy beaches with high waves are less likely to be populated... and are also the beaches where most flotsam and jetsam washes up from faraway places.

1 A stone, male or female, especially one that is suggestively shaped.

2 A shell. Break it in half. You and your lover each keep a piece as a token of your affection.

3 A piece of beach glass. This should be very smooth, no rough edges. Your lover is supposed to keep this with him or her always in a pocket or purse, to touch and feel throughout the day, a reminder of your love.

4 A flower, delivered by you as soon as it is picked, with a kiss. In Hawai'i it is perfectly permissible to pluck just one or two blossoms from shrubs or bushes growing along sidewalks or public pathways, particularly if you are giving them as a sign of affection to a lover, or welcoming a tourist.

5 A piece of coral. Old coral comes in a wonderful variety of interesting shapes and sizes. Great to use as paperweights, door stops, or as decorations for the driveway or yard. (In Hawai'i, you can remove dead coral that has washed up on a beach, but you must not take live coral from the ocean.)

6 A uniquely shaped piece of driftwood. Use your imagination. Driftwood pieces can be suggestively shaped . . . or just interesting.

7 A cutting from a flowering shrub such as hibiscus, 'ilima or bougainvillea is an especially enduring reminder of your affection. Help care for it, showcasing your nurturing nature.

8 Find a piece of coral or a shell with a circular opening. Braid a grass cord for the stone or shell and string it through to make an impromptu necklace or bracelet for your love.

9 A piece of fruit – one you've picked from a tree or garden, not purchased. Papaya, mango, oranges and guava are often available. Liliko'i – or passion fruit – is especially appropriate if you can find it, usually at higher or cooler elevations. Bring your love just one piece, not more.

10 A glass float. Clear glass balls of various sizes, used to hold up fishing nets, have always been a precious find. Fishing boats use plastic materials now and glass floats are becoming nearly extinct. If you do find one, consider yourself very lucky. It's a sign of good fortune to come. Sharing it with a friend or lover will spread that good luck.

11 A plastic float. These are larger and not nearly as attractive as the old glass floats, but still make wonderful displays on lānai or yards. They are relatively easy to find. Collect them with your love. Use a waterproof marking pen to sign and date, a reminder of your affection. 🌴

Out with old; in with the new

Only happy spirits will hover over the marriage of Beau and Brandy Geddis of Maui. At their wedding reception, Lin Watanabe, of Watanabe Taiko Drummers, helped the couple beat out any bad spirits that might be lingering and welcome in happy new spirits to guide their life together. Lin describes the traditional Japanese drumming, often seen at *bon* dances, as "taking out all the bad that's around so the new can come in." †

BOB FIJAL PHOTOS

131

A dream fulfilled

His father and mother had always longed to visit Hawai'i, and when he was a kid Wayne Peterson vowed someday he'd send his parents there. But Wayne's mother died before she could realize that wish and, by the time the family could afford the trip, Wayne's father could not bear to go without her.

Wayne grew up to be a successful graphic artist. He met his own wife, Joanne, on a blind date. They had four children and spent 25 happy years together. And all that time he remembered his parents' unfulfilled dream.

When Wayne wanted to celebrate his and Joanne's long, wedded bliss, he decided on a tribute to both loving marriages: his own and his parents. He would take Joanne to Hawai'i and there he would surprise her with a renewal of their marriage vows.

Wayne recalled a favorite Elvis Presley movie, *Blue Hawai'i*, filmed on the island of Kaua'i. And a client suggested nearby Wailua River as a romantic spot for the renewal vows. Kaua'i's many waterfalls stream down Mount Wai'ale'ale, wettest spot on earth, in silvery ribbons and collect at the state's largest river, the gentle Wailua. Here kayaks and canoes drift dreamily under overhanging boughs.

Blue Hawai'i was filmed just across the street from Smith's Tropical Paradise, a private 30-acre park bordering the river. A park spokesperson promised to have everything ready for the ceremony, followed by a public boat cruise and lū'au.

A few days before the ceremony Wayne casually took Joanne shopping at Waikīkī where he helped her choose a pretty *mu'u mu'u*. She was unaware that the traditional Hawaiian dress would be the gown for her second wedding ceremony.

"Getting Joanne to Kaua'i was easy," Wayne says. "Getting her to wear a dress for a river cruise was trickier." Joanne suspected something was up when

Wayne and Joanne, married again.

they arrived early for the boat ride and Wayne suggested they go for a walk.

"Okay. What's going on?" she asked.

"We're going to renew our wedding vows," he replied.

"Wait a minute. What if I've changed my mind? What if I don't want to renew them?" she quipped.

Wayne led her along a path past secluded gardens and lagoons, across a bridge to a lovely little island where a minister and assistant appeared. The couple recited their vows for the second time in their lives, and Wayne gave Joanne a mother's ring with birthstones representing their four children.

The first ceremony had been flavored with anxious expectations; the second was seasoned with peaceful gratitude.

The first vows had been made in front of family and friends; a variety of birds shared the second one. As a video camera captured the ceremony, a pair of curious peacocks strutted by and chickens cackled.

"It was wonderful. We named the chicken Henna B and decided she was the maid of honor and the rooster was my best man," Wayne laughs. "You could say the whole thing was for the birds."

Love birds. 🌴

The Tidepools on Maui. See page 157.

Queen's Bath; Nature's massage

There is nothing as sensuous as a massage and the 'aina, the land, provides materials for especially interesting rubs. As you drive along the southern or western coasts of the islands, look for easily-accessible secluded areas where a kind of Jacuzzi is created near the shore by lava outpourings. The lava rocks break the waves, forming quiet pools, and waves washing in provide multiple small "showers." Early Hawaiians called such natural pools "queen's baths."

You and your lover can best enjoy the natural massage of the waves early in the morning, before the sea becomes too wild. Warning: Spend at least five minutes watching the wave action before you attempt to enter the water. Stay close to shore and make sure the tide is not strong enough to pull you in or hurl you against the lava rocks.

A little island ingenuity adds to your experience. Try gathering:

♥ **Warm rocks.** Massage your lover with smooth beach stones heated by the sun. Press the flat end gently into the muscles with a circular motion.

♥ **Fresh seaweed** comes in a variety of textures and colors, all slightly slimy and sensuous. You and your lover should each take handfuls and rub the seaweed all over each other before diving into the ocean. Islanders once believed this protected your loved one from drowning or being attacked by sharks.

♥ **Fragrant leaves**, such as eucalyptus or *maile*. Crumble and rub all over your lover's skin.

♥ **Handfuls of sand** make a cleansing and stimulating massage. Gently abrasive, they help to remove old skin and blemishes.

♥ **Bits of smooth coral.** Found on some beaches, smoothly abrasive pieces of coral can be used like purchased pumice to smooth skin. Be sensitive enough to perform this act of humble love on your lover's feet and you will have his or her undying appreciation.

Now! Let the ocean waves rinse you clean. Lie there. Enjoy. Kiss your love. 🌴

Looking for love?

Hawai'i is more open and friendly than many places. Feel free to speak to anyone. In fact, it's downright rude not to meet the eye of a stranger and smile as you pass on the street, on the beach or in a shopping mall.

Here are some distinctively Hawaiian "openers" to get the conversation started:

At a farmers' market or the produce department of a grocery store:

> "Do you see any cherimoya? I've heard of it and I'd like to try it."

> "Do you have any idea how to cook eggplant?"

> "Can you tell if this pineapple is ripe?"

All of us who live here share a love of the islands.

On the beach:

> "What a gorgeous day! It sure is hard to work when you live in Hawai'i"

or "I bet it's hard to work when you live in Hawai'i!"

> "You are in such good shape! Do you belong to a paddling club?"

Many of us have moved here from somewhere else. The experience gives us a common curiosity:

> "Where are you from originally?"

> "How long have you lived here?"

> "Did you have any difficulty finding work here?"

> "Was it difficult for you to make the decision to come here?" 🌴

Great (cheap) dates on Oʻahu

Here are suggestions from several Oʻahu singles for romantic free or cheap dates. Some ideas are applicable to any island.

- ♥ **Walk.** Take a moonlight walk, scheduled regularly at Waimea Falls Park (638-8511) or the Honolulu Zoo (971-7195). Under a full moon, parks assume a wondrous appearance. Sign up. Call the Nature Conservancy (537-4508) and ask for hiking and nature walk schedules.

- ♥ **Be romantic.** Stroll on any beach. Pick up a pretty shell or a piece of coral and offer it to your date as a souvenir. Or, tell your date you are taking it home as a reminder of the beginning of your relationship.

- ♥ **Check the Honolulu Weekly** or the entertainment and community sections of newspapers for free concerts or lectures. Choose any subject that will interest both of you. A lecture on relationships can be especially appropriate and provide topics of conversation.

- ♥ **Park.** The tops of Tantalus or Pacific Heights are great for enjoying the view. Or, drive out to the windward side of the island. Have a sunset dinner at the Crouching Lion Inn, then park out at Laʻie Point. Watch the waves, talk and get to know each other.

- ♥ **Hike.** Get up early (5 a.m. or so) and drive to Makapuʻu lighthouse with backpacks full of fruit, water and food. Hike up to the lighthouse and watch the sun come up. Then hike over the cliff to the inlet and dive off the rock or bask in the sun. Or, trek up to Kapena Falls off the Pali Highway. Or, try the easy hike up Makiki.

- ♥ **Picnic.** Kaʻena Point Nature Preserve has sand dunes, endemic coastal plants, albatross nests, whale watching. Or, rent kayaks, take along a lunch, and paddle to Mokulua islet off Lanikai/Kailua.

- ♥ **Enjoy free or inexpensive shows and entertainment.** Hawaiʻi's many performers appear at Borders Book Stores, on shopping center stages, and in inexpensive resort shows and lounges. Perfect for a casual date.

- ♥ **Be spontaneous.** Call at 4 p.m. and suggest the two of you go down to the beach to watch the sunset at 6. Bring a bottle of champagne or wine and two glasses. As an extra touch, wrap the bottle in a flower *lei*.

Keeping in touch

Living far from your lover? Here are two touching ways to keep in touch.

Insert packets of purchased flower or vegetable seeds into your card or letter to your lover. Enclose a note:

1 *This is for us to plant when we are together.*

or

2 *Plant this, think of me, and by the time it sprouts, we will be together.*

To let your lover know you are thinking of your good times together, correspond often. Cards, notes, short letters. Each time, enclose a $1 bill in your correspondence and ask your lover to set up an "Us Together" account. The money will be for a fancy dinner when the two of you are together. 🌴

A truly romantic restaurant is sunsets and moonbeams, candles and kisses. It's much . . .

More than a menu

A dancer at LaMariana

Few places on earth have as many romantic restaurants as Hawai'i and, thanks to our cultural mix, you can take your love on an imaginary trip to almost any place in the world: Thailand, Greece, Africa, Switzerland as well as Italy, Japan and China. Why not signal your intent to take your lover "around the world" – in the dining sense – for dinner in a different country each week for, perhaps, three or four months.

A visit to a fine restaurant can be as romantic and festive as you decide to make it. If you are celebrating a special occasion, advance planning is essential. Share your plans with the manager or *maitre d'* and ask for suggestions.

Arrange to have the restaurant's musicians play your love's favorite song or a melody that means the most to both of you. Corny? Hawai'i is a romantic, broad-minded culture where nothing that comes sincerely from the heart is considered corny.

Our favorite romantic restaurants, chosen mostly for ambiance, happen to serve mostly traditional Hawaiian/American fare–freshly caught fish, crispy salads, fruit. They follow:

Romantic restaurants

Hawai'i (Big Island)

Edwards at Kanaloa. Your table is set between the ocean and a shimmering pool, both reflecting the moon. Edwards, on the ocean in Keauhuou, offers gourmet food using local ingredients and spices. Delightful contradictions: the atmosphere is casual, but the service is elegant. The price is costly, but not unaffordable. (808) 322-1434.

O'ahu

LaMariana Restaurant & Bar. With blowfish lights, fishing nets and glass floats, this cozy place on Ke'ehi Lagoon looks like the set of a 1940s movie. LaMariana snuggles next to a sailboat harbor in Honolulu's industrial area, where few tourists find it. Live music is featured almost every night and local entertainment on weekends. Take Sand Island Access Road off Nimitz Highway south of the airport, travel about a quarter mile, past Kilgos hardware store and watch for a small sign on your right. Follow the road and watch for the restaurant entrance on your left. Reservations recommended weekends. (808) 848-2800.

Moloka'i

Kaluako'i Hotel's dining room overlooks the ocean and the service is so friendly you'll feel you're visiting family...which may not be your idea of a romantic dinner. But a stroll through the torch-lit hotel grounds after dinner provides the romantic ambiance. (808) 552-2555.

Maui

The Garden Restaurant at Kapalua Bay Hotel. Schedule a sunset dinner at this restaurant with open walls overlooking gardens to Kapalua Bay. Have a drink, listen to live piano music and watch the sun set over the island of Moloka'i. Then meander through a scrumptious seafood buffet (Friday and Saturday nights). The service is impeccable, the candlelight romantic, the entertainment (usually a solo singer) low-keyed and relaxing. And the price is reasonable – for Maui. Reservations a must. (808) 669-5656.

Kaua'i

Tidepools at Hyatt Regency, Kaua'i, Poipū. Kaua'i is so beautiful and unspoiled that sunset at any oceanfront restaurant is romantic. But Tidepools offers some extra ambiance: thatched huts, stone floors, lots of rattan and soft lights, very Polynesian. Prices are reasonable. (808) 742-1234.

Lāna'i

Hotel Lāna'i. There are two much more elegant hotels on this tiny island, but we like the cozy, rustic feeling of this small old lodge with its stone hearth. Located right on Lāna'i City's quaint town green, it's surrounded by tall Cook pines. The food's not gourmet, but the servings are hearty. Prices are reasonable. (808) 565-4700. 🌴

MATTHEW THAYER PHOTO

Food flirting

When you were a child, your parents told you not to play with your food. You are a grown-up now, and guess what? Playing with food can be sensuous fun.

Hawai'i's juicy, pulpy fruits seem to have been made to eat sensuously. Golden red mango, cut into slippery soft pieces; *liliko'i* (passionfruit) sliced in half, its slimy center waiting to be taken; guava, so softly pink and full of seeds; papaya, fragrant and vulnerable; pineapple, strong and sharp against the tongue; and banana... well, banana leaves little to the imagination.

Food flirting can be as innocently thoughtful as cutting up a plate of fruit for your lover and feeding it slowly, piece by piece, as you lie on a beach under a palm tree or in a hammock on your *lānai*.

Food flirting can also be boldly seductive— sending a handsome stranger across a crowded airplane a message by looking at him and slowly, almost nonchalantly, licking a drop of guava nectar from your lips.

One Hawai'i visitor describes an especially sensuous rendevous she enjoyed in these islands. Her lover awoke her each morning by gently drizzling orange juice on her lips.

142

Techno-love

Whether you and your love are separated by an ocean, or just a few blocks, access to email is a relationship boon. Just don't let the boon become a bother. Make sure email use is okay with the boss and access to messages is for your lover's eyes only. Here's how to make your email more romantic:

1 Send short messages at unlikely times throughout the day:
8 a.m.: thought of you.
10 a.m: thought of you again.
Noon: Longing for you.

2 Remember a happy moment:
I saw a child skipping rope and I thought of last Saturday when you jumped up and down with joy . . .

3 Quote just two lines from a romantic poem:
How do I love thee? Let me count the ways.
"I love you to the depth and breadth and height my soul can reach."

4 Write your own:
A sandy beach, a whispering wave, a glowing sunset – and you. Those are the things I long for throughout my day.

5 Or make up a silly rhyme:
I love you more than mango, more than lilikoi – You're my wahine, I'm your Hawai'i boy.
Plumeria is white, hibiscus is red; Right now I'd rather be with you, in bed! 🌴

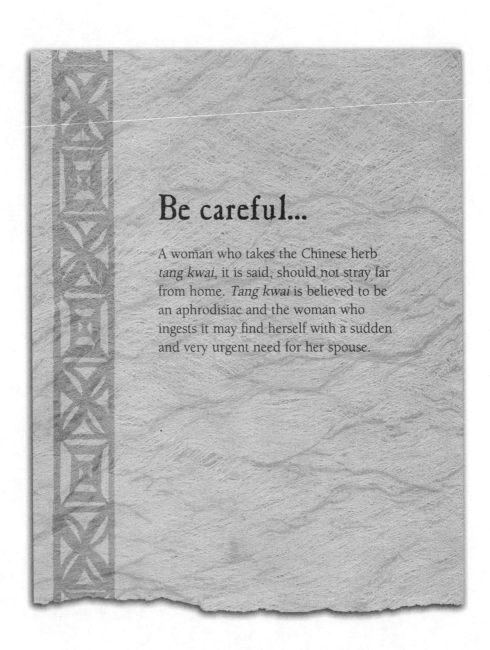

Be careful...

A woman who takes the Chinese herb *tang kwai*, it is said, should not stray far from home. *Tang kwai* is believed to be an aphrodisiac and the woman who ingests it may find herself with a sudden and very urgent need for her spouse.

TONI POLANCY PHOTO

Romantic beaches

If you live on these islands, chances are your social life has long centered on the beaches. Beach parks are the place for family celebrations, for get-togethers with friends, for hearty exercise like swimming and surfing, and for quiet times of reflection.

Secret, quiet beaches are another genre. Locations for quiet contemplation or private encounters, they are the very best places to court, to have romantic times together – whether those times be mentally or sexually exciting.

Here are our favorites, divided into two types: romantic secret beaches and nude beaches. Be sure to sample a variety of these sandy and/or rocky pleasures.

Beach 69, The Big Island (Hawai'i)

This is actually Wai'alea Bay beach in the Kohala area (northwestern part) of the Big Island, and it bears its intriguing nickname because a utility pole with the number 69 marks the turnoff for the beach. Watch for the pole on Route 19 near another great spot, the lovingly landscaped Hāpuna Beach State Park.

Palauea Beach, Maui

A small forest of *kiawe* shelters this wide white sand beach and its breathtaking view across to Kaho'olawe Island. Just past the exotic white Kea Lani Hotel at Wailea in South Maui, take the road *makai* (toward the ocean), turn left at the bottom and travel a few hundred yards. Exquisite, but rapidly being sold off to private parties.

Hanalei and Hā'ena beaches, Kaua'i

Just driving to the beaches of northern Kaua'i is romantic. Motor to Hā'ena Beach (or any of the beaches past Hanalei) the morning after a rainfall. Ribbons of glistening water pour off the cliffs around Hanalei Valley and your heart (and your lover's too) will turn over at the sheer beauty. Keep driving beyond Hanalei as far as the road goes and you'll pass lovely beaches that make you gasp: Can this be real? Or are we in a movie set? (You might well be ... Kaua'i is often the setting for movies. In the film *South Pacific*, Nellie Forbush sang that man right out of her hair along Ha'ena Beach. You've already passed Anahola, where *King Kong* hung from the cliffs and Harrison Ford hid from pirates in *Six Days, Seven Nights*.)

Lāna'i: Pu'u Pehe Cove

Twenty-foot cliffs surrounding a golden-sand cove make for plenty of privacy. And if that isn't enough, Sweetheart Rock, a heart-shaped formation, is nearby. This is on the southern end of little Lāna'i. From Lāna'i City travel Mānele Road to its end and head right. 🌴

A kiss at Kahana Bay

Is a kiss really more memorable when it happens in a romantic backdrop like Kahana Bay, O'ahu? Yes, say Mike Daak and Judy Bowes. Soon to wed, the couple will reside on tiny Midway Island, where Mike is a systems specialist.

Kahana Bay, O'ahu

The most beautiful beach on O'ahu is Kahana Bay. Travel Kamehameha Highway past Kane'ohe on the windward side. Keep going past Ka'a'awa and the *pali* (cliff) highway takes a wide curve to the left. You come suddenly upon the half moon of Kahana Bay, ringed with palm trees and looking like a delicate painting. Fewer people clutter these beaches than those on the North Shore or Waikīkī. Stop, admire and swim (carefully, of course!). 🌴

TONI POLANCY PHOTOS

A trip to Lā'ie

Lā'ie Beach, below famous Lā'ie Point, is one of O'ahu's most beautiful and deserted beaches. There are two ways to get to Lā'ie Beach. Drive Kamehameha Highway on the windward side of O'ahu to Lā'ie town. Just past the Polynesian Cultural Center on your left, watch for a small road curving around the bay on your right that looks more like a driveway. It will appear just before you see the Lā'ie Shopping Center on your left. Turn right on the road and follow it to its end. Or, to visit Lā'ie Point, turn right on the road directly across from the shopping center, head up the hill and turn right again at the top. That road will lead you to the point, especially exciting when the ocean is rough and spray splashes over rock formations. Our favorite way to Lā'ie Beach is via this upper road. On the right side of the road as you head up, watch for the path marked by the sign post. Follow the path to the steps leading down to the beach.

Winsome model Heidi Van Der Veer leads you "down the garden path" to the beach. 🌴

Diamond Head Beach

Nude beaches

The islands are well-known for a liberal attitude toward clothing – appropriate since ancient Hawaiians wore little or none. However, these days it is illegal to take off your clothes in a public place. Police occasionally, though rarely, raid the beaches. Officially, there are no nude beaches in Hawai'i. Unofficially, every resident can recite the location of clothing-optional stretches of sand, and we've listed a few here.

Secret Beach, Kaua'i

A secluded golden sand beach next to tall cliffs, near majestic Kīlauea Lighthouse, Secret Beach is the loveliest nude beach in the state and would fit equally well under our "romantic beaches" category. From Kaua'i's main highway, Route 56, turn *makai* (toward the ocean) toward the lighthouse at Kīlauea. Turn left at Kauapea Road. The first dirt road on the right leads to the beach trail. Drive through to the end and park. Walk toward the ocean, through small pastures and fields. Then head down a steep path to the beach. If you have trouble finding it, ask any neighbor.

Little Beach, Maui

Big waves here; watch your equipment. Follow Wailea Alanui Road through Wailea Resort in South Kīhei and keep going until you reach Mākena Beach State Park and park your car in the first of two big lots. Walk the few feet to the beach and look to your right. That hump of dirt and rock is Puʻu ʻŌlaʻi. Follow the path to scramble over it and you'll look down at Little Beach – and all those people! (Part of the path is sometimes under water during high tides, but still accessible).

Poʻolau Bay, Molokaʻi

One of many secluded places on this very quiet island. Go south to Kaluakoʻi. Turn right at Pōhauloa Road and right again at Kulawai Place.

Diamond Head, Oʻahu

Hard to believe people take their clothes off on any of Oʻahu's crowded beaches. But, there's a popular gay beach to the north (or left) of the lighthouse below Diamond Head. And people allegedly remove their clothes occasionally on some secluded parts of Kailua Beach and Lanikai Beach in Windward Oʻahu.

Honokōhau Beach, Big Island

Salt and pepper sand that sticks to the buns. Just south of the Kona airport, take the paved road between the 97 and 98 mile markers to Honokōhau Harbor. Park and walk north.

Kehena Beach, The Big Island

This beautiful black sand beach four miles north of lava-destroyed Kalapana on the Puna coast, is worth looking for. First, study the history of this volcano-threatened area. You and your love, sensitive souls that you are, will surely feel the *mana* and be awed by the perseverance of Puna's residents. On Route 137, find the trail near the 19 mile marker on the highway and scramble down. 🌴

Alone with the roar of Wailua Falls near Kipahulu, Maui.

Jane and Len Sutton at the Falls at Kulaniapia

Romantic get-aways

What makes a weekend get-away or honeymoon spot romantic? First, privacy. Second, ambiance. Third, pampering.

Big Island

HILO SIDE: **The Inn at Kulaniapia** is a small bed and breakfast next to two waterfalls, occasionally rented out to film companies. Its 22 lush, secluded acres, just 10 minutes from Hilo, provide perfect spots for intimacy. Have a close encounter with your love near a 120-foot waterfall or swim in the 300-foot-wide pool at its base. Or stop to express your affection near the Waiau River. Take turns applying the mosquito repellent on each other and who knows what will happen. Very reasonably priced.

(808) 966-6373 or (800) 838-6373 www.waterfall.net

KONA SIDE: At **Kona Village**, thatched cottages, some of them on stilts over the water, recreate authentic Hawai'i. There are elevated walkways to the ocean shore and only 115 *hale* (houses) hidden on an immense 82 acres just north of the airport. Everyone gets together for *lū'au*, probably the most authentic on the Big Island. Anti-dress code, casualness is a must... but there's nothing casual about the cost. Expensive.
(808) 325-5555, (800) 367-5290 or www.konavillage.com

O'ahu

Kahala Mandarin Oriental Hawaii. A favorite hotel for weddings, the Hotel Mandarin Oriental, in a quiet beachfront setting near Diamond Head, is perfect for an I-don't-want-to-leave-our-room weekend. Expect pampering at this relatively small Asian hotel in Honolulu's exclusive Kahala district. Spacious, posh rooms with elegant marble dressing/bath rooms designed for two. Some suites are set cozily around a dolphin pool. The creatures leap just a few feet from your lāna'i. Long late breakfasts, great lunch buffets and perfect evening dining without leaving the grounds. And easy accessibility to Waikīkī if you do crave a different excitement. Expensive, but worth it. *Kama'āina* rates are sometimes available.
(808) 739-8888 or www.mandarin-oriental.com

Maui

Hotel Hana Maui. Famous people come here to share quiet time with lovers and families; why shouldn't you? Expect elegance and luxury at this hotel in the middle of a remote, incredibly lush rural village. Conduct your own tour of Hana's many waterfalls, most of them swimmable. And when you get back to the hotel, you and your *ku'u ipo* (my sweetheart) can relax in your own outdoor hot tub. Expensive? Yes, but you deserve pampering. (800) 321-HANA or www.hotelhanamaui.com

Kauaʻi

Waimea Plantation Cottages. Here's Hawaiʻi as most people imagine it: little houses set amidst lush tropical foliage. Old plantation managers' cottages were moved from neighboring cane fields and meticulously restored to make this a very charming getaway.

Waimea Plantation Cottages

Waimea is on the very quiet, still untouristy side of the island, toward Kokeʻe State Park and Waimea Canyon. Each cabin has a kitchen, and there's also the Waimea Brewing Co., an *ono* (delicious) restaurant, for lunch and dinner. Reasonable. (800) 992-4632 or www.waimea-plantation.com.

Lānaʻi

The Lodge at Kōʻele. Set among tall pines, the lodge looks like it belongs in the English countryside. Quiet, elegant and the service is impeccable. Tee off with your love or use a jeep to bounce down to secret beaches on this tiny island. Very expensive. (800) 321-4666 or www.lanai-resorts.com.

Molokaʻi

Hotel Molokaʻi. Molokaʻi is as close as you'll get to the Hawaiian life of 50 or 60 years ago… and most of Molokaʻi's fewer than 7,000 residents strive to keep things simple. Here's the place for quiet privacy if you don't need much outside activity. Hotel Molokaʻi, near the old town of Kaunakakai, is earthy and friendly. And inexpensive. (808) 553-5347 or www.hotelmolokai.com. 🌴

Take a hike to some secret places

Walking and hiking will take you to the islands' most incredible places: to crashing waterfalls with cooling pools, to lookouts with majestic views, or to secret coves with private beaches.

Some of these romantic locations require only a short walk; others demand hours of hiking on lava fields or through rain forests. The trips are wonderfully rewarding – but remember that Hawai'i can also be dangerous: Steep volcanic valleys, monster waves, and ever-changing tides and weather patterns.

Use common sense: If it is raining or has been raining in the past few days, don't attempt mountain hikes or enter narrow valleys where rock slides or flash floods can occur with no warning.

Be sure to carry enough food to get you through a night if you become stranded and also take plenty of water whenever you go on any outing. Stay on known trails, where searchers can find you if you become lost or stranded. Don't wander into secluded areas – inadvertently visiting someone's *pakalōlō* (marijuana) patch can be deadly.

Remember beaches that appear calm at one time of the day can be crashing with waves that eat up sand (and people) at other times. And not all waters are safe for swimming – any rough surf is better left to professionals.

That said – here are some of the most romantic walks and hikes you'll find anywhere in the world. Some, like the trip to Maui's Swinging Bridges and a swim in Kaua'i's Blue Room, are dangerous and *kapu*, forbidden. Be sure to heed warning signs and no trespassing signs and get owners' permissions before crossing posted lands.

Our favorite strolls:

156

Maui

The Tidepools

The ride on Honoapiʻilani Highway past Kapalua in northwestern Maui is breathtaking and exciting even without a stop at Tidepools. But if the ocean is calm, about ten miles past Kapalua resort look for a huge egg-shaped rock to your left. Park your car and scramble down the little path to the ocean. You'll see deep, calm tidepools and a wonderfully romantic "tub," usually private, in which to relax together.

Hike level: very easy, but make sure the ocean is calm.

Mānoa Falls Trail – Oʻahu

Swinging Bridges

Take Route 340 south of Kahului or Wailuku. After you pass the village of Waiheʻe, slow down and watch for Waiheʻe Valley Road, a left-hand turn just before the bridge. Follow the road to its end. You'll find a cleared parking area. Lock your car and head up the path. An old, still-used irrigation system marks most of the way. On this easy, approximately one-hour hike, you'll trek across two cable "swinging bridges" over creek beds and traverse a bamboo forest. Follow the path until you reach the wide, high "waterfall" created by the irrigation system. The falls form a large pool of clear water that you'll relish after the warm hike, and plenty of other secluded nooks and crannies in which to relax and talk.

Hike level: moderate, about one hour each way.

Kauaʻi

The Blue Room

The Blue Room, near the North Shore, is actually a volcanic cave within a cave. There's a large pool at the first, open cave. The Blue Room is a small cave at the back of the cavern. Its interior glows with phosphorus and is particularly bright when the sun shines just right, from 2 to 4 p.m., locals say. To find the Blue Room, swim toward the right side of the back of the big pool. The shadowy rock makes it scary – and at least one person has died in the pool's deep, dark waters, so don't try this unless you are a very confident swimmer. Even if you decide not to swim, the cave is worth visiting. Best reached by driving past Princeville to Hāʻena Beach Park at the end of Highway 56 and then doubling back about a quarter mile. Pass the cave on your right that you can see from the road (it's not the one you want), slow down and pull into the next small parking area, marked by a sign. Park and follow the path up a few yards, staying to your right.
Hike level: very easy, but the swim takes nerve and knowledge.

Māhāʻulepū

The half-moon curve of Māhāʻulepū Beach, in a small bay, is surrounded by rock walls and crashing waves on both sides, yet remains relatively calm. Getting there is quite a challenge – it's a very easy walk, but a bit difficult to find. At the Hyatt Regency at Poʻipū, follow Poʻipū Road past the golf course and the stables, until the road ends. Park and sign a release form in the cabin here, then start hiking the trail toward the ocean and follow it along the ocean cliffs for about half a mile. You'll see the beach, a sheltered cove below. Don't try to bathe nude here – you are visible to the horseback riders on the cliffs up above.
Hike level: moderate. Very dry, take plenty of drinking water.

Oʻahu

Mālaekahana State Park

This large park on windward Oʻahu is about halfway up the eastern side of the island at 56-335 Kamehameha Highway, just past Lāʻie – and several worlds away from busy, commercial Waikīkī. With rustic ironwood trees and plenty of space to picnic and camp, Mālaekahana is reminiscent of state parks in the Pacific Northwest.

The long, narrow beach is nearly deserted on weekdays. Wade over to Goat Island, a bird sanctuary with a quiet beach cove. Overnight camping is also permitted at the park. Nearby cabins are rented up to a year in advance for weekends and holidays, but if you are coming during the week you may find one available. Call Friends of Māleakahana, a non-profit group, at 808-293-1736. *Hike level: almost none . . . just a shady walk.*

Mānoa Valley and Lyon Arboretum

HEIDI VAN DE VEER PHOTO

Mānoa Falls – Lyon Arboretum

You'll caress under a rainbow at Mānoa Valley. The large, lush, misty valley (*Mānoa* means vast), just behind the University of Hawai'i, is often adorned by a bright rainbow, arching across the valley. Follow Mānoa Valley Road, past quaint old houses, until it ends at Paradise Park and the Lyon Arboretum. Ignore the first parking area and go up to the second or third. Park and follow the trail deep into the forested Ko'olau mountains. Look at ribbons of light shining through tall, vine-covered trees. Stop, breathe deeply, and kiss your love. The other hikers will not only understand – they'll probably applaud. Then traipse the 20-minute hike to Mānoa Falls and pool. Breathtaking! And this less than 15 minutes from the University of Hawai'i exit off Honolulu's H-1 Freeway. *Hike level: easy to medium.*

Big Island

Waimanu Valley

What could be more romantic than nature's own movie set? Waimanu Valley in the Big Island's northern Waipi'o Valley area was featured in the film *Waterworld*. It seems too magical to be real, but Waimanu Valley is exactly as pictured – lush, pristine, very remote – and well worth the four-mile hike through forested trails. This hike takes all day one way, so plan to spend the night. Call the state Forestry and Wildlife division a month in advance for free permits and maps. Phone numbers are at the end of this section. *Hike level: strenuous.*

Halapē Beach

Get naked with the turtles at remote, golden-sanded Halapē beach – but first plan on a hot, dry five-hour backpacking trip that will leave you eager to enter the cooling sea. The Halapē trail, about 14.5 miles round trip, starts at Volcanoes National Park, where you'll register to spend the night at the Halapē beach shelter. This is a romantically spooky spot. In 1975 an earthquake caused a tidal wave that wiped out the coconut grove at the shore and left upside down trunks known as the Tiki Halapē. Cuddle close to your love. Watch out for Night Marchers, ghosts of long dead *ali'i* (chiefs) who tramp through this part of the Big Island at night in full dress. Call the state forestry division for maps and details. *Hike level: very tough.*

Moloka'i

Moa'ula Falls

The three-mile trek to Moa'ula Falls in Eastern Moloka'i is muddy and mosquito-plagued, but worth the repellent. You'll pass through bananas, mangos and taro in a quiet setting and within an hour hear the sound of the falls. Legend says a giant lizard lives in the beautiful deep pool and occasionally eats swimmers. Place a leaf upon the pool's waters. If it floats, the lizard wants you to swim. If it doesn't, better stay out of the water. Get forestry maps; see phone numbers at end of this section. *Hike level: moderate.*

Pāpōhaku Beach

The three-mile-long hike (one way) of lovely (and lonely) Pāpōhaku Beach on western Moloka'i is very romantic and non-exhausting.

160

Crashing shorelines (look, don't try to swim), beautiful views of distant O'ahu and wide, uninterrupted expanses of white sand as well as plenty of *kiawe* trees to shelter you. Take a blanket – *kiawe* can be prickly. Just follow Route 460 west to Kaluako'i Road. You'll find the beach – it's huge. *Hike level: very easy.*

Kalaupapa National Historic Park

You'll long remember a trip together to Kalaupapa, the world-renowned former leper colony. Kalaupapa, a national park, is really a shrine to the thousands of Hansen's Disease

Friends cool off at Alele Falls, Kaipo, Maui.

sufferers who once were banished to this isolated peninsula. What's romantic about this place? Visiting the village, hearing its stories, is an emotional experience that will leave you loving and appreciating your own good fortunes – and each other. You can hike down the very steep cliffs; fly into the peninsula by plane; or choose another popular way – a mule ride. Call Damien Tours (808) 567-6171 or Rare Adventures (808) 567-6088. *Hike level: incredibly difficult. Ride, don't walk.*

Detailed maps of hikes are available from the Foresty and Wildlife Division.

Call:
O'ahu: (808) 587-0166
Big Island: (808) 974-4221
Maui: (808) 984-8100
Kaua'i: (808) 274-3433

Advertise your love

The first time Roland "R.K." Harper laid eyes on Kathleen "Moloka'i" Kehlor, she was painting actors' faces for a performance of "*Pippin*" at the Army Community Theater on O'ahu. A few months later, R.K. and Moloka'i sat under a banyan tree at Ala Moana Beach Park in Honolulu, reserving a picnic table for a cast party, and chatting. And love began to blossom.

When a fire displaced R.K. just a few weeks later, Kathleen unselfishly invited him to stay with her and her sister until he found a new home. That was in 1982. The couple, happily "Serving each other's needs" ever since, have repeatedly proven those formal wedding vows: "For richer; for poorer" and "in sickness, in health" before ever taking them. They survived tight financial times early in their relationship and a severe illness that hospitalized R.K. in 1998.

On Valentine's Day 1999, R.K. proposed on one knee under the same banyan tree where they had first conversed. They were married in 1999 at the Star of the Sea Catholic Church in Kahala, O'ahu. A year later, he was still declaring his undying love--this time via an ad in the newspaper that surprised and delighted his bride. 🌴

Bibliography *and suggested reading*

(Many of these titles are out of date and impossible to purchase, but most are available through the Hawai'i state library system.)

Becoming Tongan, An Ethnography of Childhood by Helen Morton copyright 1996 by University of Hawaii Press

Bed the Turtle Softly: Legends of the South Paciic by Mary Edith and Joel S. Branham copyright 1975 by Mary Edith and Joel S. Branham

Captain James Cook by Alan Villiers copyright 1967 by Alan Villiers

Friendly Isles, A Tale Of Tonga by Patricia Ledyard copyright 1974 by Patricia Matheson. Printed in Great Britain by William Clowes and Son Ltd. Reprinted in Tonga at the government printing office, Nuku'alofa

Great Sailor: A life of the discoverer Capt. James Cook by John W. Vandercook copyright 1951 by The Dial Press

Growing Native Hawaiian Plants by Heidi Leianuenue Bornhorst copyright 1996 by The Bess Press, Inc.

Hanahana: An Oral History Anthology of Hawai'i's Working People by Michi Kodama-Nishimoto, Warren S. Nishimoto and Cynthia A. Oshiro copyright 1984 by Ethnic Studies Oral History Project, University of Hawai'i at Mānoa

Hawai'i: An Uncommon History by Edward Joesting copyright 1972 by W. W. Norton & Company, Inc.

Hawai'i's Queen Liliuokalani by Adrienne Stone copyright 1947 by Adrienne Stone. Published by Julian Messenger, New York

Hawai'i's Story by Hawai'i's Queen Liliuokalani copyright 1990 by Mutual Publishing, Honolulu

Hawai'i: the Sugar-Coated Fortress by Francine du Plessix Gray copyright 1972 by Francine du Plessix Gray

Hawai'i: Truth Stranger than Fiction by LaRue W. Piercy copyright 1985 by LaRue W. Piercy

Hawaiian Religion & Magic by Scott Cunningham copyright 1994 by Llewellyn Publications, St. Paul, MN

163

Hawaiian Mythology by Martha Beckwith copyright 1970 by University of Hawai'i Press. Originally published in 1940 by Yale University Press for the Folklore Foundation of Vassar College

I Married A Prince by Myrtle King Kaapu copyright 1977 by Myrtle King Kaapu

Jan Ken Po: the World of Hawai'i's Japanese Americans by Dennis M. Ogawa copyright by The Japanese American Research Center

Kahuna La'au Lapa'au by June Gutmanis copyright 1976 by Island Heritage Publishing

Maori Marriage: An Essay in Reconstruction by Bruce Briggs, copyright 1960 by Bruce Biggs. Reprinted in 1970

Maui's Mitte and The General: A glimpse into the lives of Mr. And Mrs. Frank Fowler Baldwin by Irma Gerner Burns copyright 1991 by John C. Baldwin

Memories of Duke: the Legend Comes to Life by Sandra Kimberly Hall and Greg Ambrose copyright 1995 by The Bess Pess, Inc., Honolulu

Of Andagi and Sanshin: Okinawan Culture in Hawai'i copyright by Hui O Laulima, Kaneohe

'Olelo No 'Eau: Hawaiian Proverbs & Poetical Sayings by Mary Kawena Pukui copyright Bishop Museum Press, Honolulu, Hawai'i

Once, A Lotus Garden and Other Stories by Jessica Saiki copyright 1987 by Jessica Saiki. Published by New River Press

Out of This Struggle: the Filipinos in Hawai'i edited by Luis B. Teodoro, Jr. copyright 1981 by University Press of Hawai'i

Pau Hana: Plantation Life and Labor in Hawai'i copyright by Ronald Takaki, University of Hawai'i Press

Pauahi: the Kamehameha Legacy by George S. Kanahele copyright 1966 by Kamehameha Schools Press

People and Cultures of Hawai'i, A Psychocultural Profile by John F. McDermott, Jr., Wen-Shing Tseng and Thomas W. Maretzki copyright 1980 by The University Press of Hawai'i

Pohaku: Hawaiian Stones a booklet by June Gutmanis copyright 1986 by the

164

Institute for Polynesian Studies, Brigham Young University, Lāʻie, Hawaiʻi

Princess of the Night Rides and other tales by John Dominis Holt copyright 1977 by John Dominis Holt. Topgallant Publishing Co., Honolulu.

Princess Pauahi Bishop and Her Legacy by Cobey Black and Kathleen Dickenson Mellen copyright 1965 by The Kamehameha Schools, Honolulu, Hawaiʻi.

Stories of Hawaii by Jack London copyright 1965 by A. Grove Day

Stories of Long Ago by Ida Elizabeth Knudsen Von Holt copyright 1985 by Daughters of Hawaiʻi (Privately printed in 1953 and 1968 by the Star-Bulletin Printing Company, Honolulu)

Tales of Molokai: the Voice of Harriet Ne collected by Gloria L. Cronin copyright 1992 by The Institute for Polynesian Studies, University of Hawaiʻi

The Filipinos in Hawaiʻi: the first 75 years copyright 1981 by Hawaiʻi Filipino News Specialty Publications, Honolulu

The Japanese in Hawaiʻi: A Century of Struggle by Roland Kotani copyright 1985 by Roland Kotani for the Oʻahu Kanyaku Imin Centennial Committee by the Hawaiʻi Hochi, Ltd., Honolulu

The Life of Captain James Cook by Arthur Kitson copyright 1911 by John Murray, London.

The Richest Girl in the World: The Exravagant Life and Fast Times of Doris Duke by Stephanie Mansfield copyright 1992 by Stephanie Mansfield. Published by G. P. Putnam's Sons, New York

Tonga by Nancy Keller and Deanna Swaney copyright 1998 by Lonely Planet, Australia

Traditions for Living: a Booklet of Chinese Customs and Folk Practices in Hawaiʻi edited by May Lee Chung, Dorothy Jim Luke and Margaret Leong Lau copyright 1979 by the Associated Chinese University Women, Honolulu

Trust No One: The Glamorous Life and Bizarre Death of Doris Duke copyright 1997 by Ted Schwarz and Tom Rybak. Printed by St. Martin's Press, New York.

Vignettes of Old Hawaiʻi by David Free copyright by Crossroads Press, Inc., Honolulu

Women's Voices in Hawaiʻi by Joyce Chapman Lebra copyright 1991 University Press of Colorado

About
the author

As a reporter, editor and columnist for newspapers in Pennsylvania and Florida, Toni Polancy covered news stories that ranged from murder to meatballs and politics to polygamy. She won many awards and held several titles, from cub reporter to managing editor of the *Erie* (Pennsylvania) *Daily Times*.

As she ascended the wobbly corporate ladder, Polancy was climbing farther and farther from her first love, writing. By 1991, her 10-hour workdays had become a series of business meetings and she did what many other middle-agers consider doing: look for stimulating change. Hawai'i beckoned, but the islands had a nasty reputation for luring newcomers only to cast them adrift on a treacherous sea of high prices, low wages and scarce jobs – so Polancy brought her own business. She established successful real estate magazines on Maui and Kaua'i.

The idea for *Hawai'i in Love* came while she was researching her first book, *So You Want to Live in Hawai'i*. The editors of that successful guide suggested she drop a section on romance as "too trivial" for a serious book. Polancy maintained that many people are drawn to these islands for romantic reasons, that our love interests often determine our lives. The romance chapter stayed and the overwhelming interest in that chapter spurred this book.

"Our continuing interest in romance and its influence fascinates me," Polancy says. "Who we love, and how, dominates our lives. Some people find love easily; others seek it all their lives and never find love. I've talked to people in their 90s who grow starry-eyed remembering romance."

Mahalo...

To Germaine Bacalso and Kaponoai Molitau, 'Ulalena, Maui Myth and Magic Theatre *performers, who modeled for the cover and photos. To* 'Ulalena *general manager John Dudley and president Roy Tokujo for their cooperation.*

To Matthew Thayer, photo-journalist in the greatest sense of the word, for loving his work.

To Rosemary Widener and Michael Nation for their endless patience in the production of this book.

To Bob Fijal for his encouragement.

To Francine Godzwa, Heidi Van Der Veer, Kekoa Kaapu, Christine Flanagan, Sandy Cessna, Jonathan Scheuer, Meg Skellenger and Dr. Sandra Ritz who edited and commented on stories during the two years it took to produce this book;

To Jody van Aalst at Island Bookshelf, Inc. who so carefully researched accent marks for the Hawaiian words.

To the staff at the Hawai'i State Archives and the Bishop Museum archives for dragging out all those files, cheerfully.

To Mary, who would not let her own story be told, but led me to others.

To a dear friend who confided that she had one regret in an otherwise fulfilling life: that she had not a great love affair, for reminding me how important love is.

To order another copy of *Hawai'i In Love* or other Barefoot
Publishing Co. books, send check or money order to:

Barefoot Publishing

P.O. Box 1017

Kihei, HI 96753

Hawai'i In Love

A history of the islands through their true love stories

Name _____

Address _____

City, State, Zip _____

Phone _____

Please send me _____ copies @ $15.95 *per book* $ _____

+ $4.00 *per book* (s/h) $ _____

Canada, please add $6 per book   **TOTAL: $ _____**

So You Want to Live in Hawai'i

A guide to settling and succeeding in the islands

Name _____

Address _____

City, State, Zip _____

Phone _____

Please send me _____ copies @ $19.95 *per book* $ _____

+ $4.00 *per book* (s/h) $ _____

TOTAL: $ _____

Canada, please add $6 per book